Case #1:
The Mary Ellen Wilson Files

By Eric A. Shelman
&
Stephen Lazoritz, M.D.

Case #1:
The Mary Ellen Wilson Files

Eric A. Shelman *and*
Stephen Lazoritz, M.D.

Forewords
By Stephen S. Zawistowski
And by Elbridge T. Gerry III
And Elbridge T. Gerry, Jr.,
with Joseph Gleason

ISBN: 978-0-9849255-3-7

This book is dedicated to Linda Shelman and Mary Lazoritz, the wonderful wives of the authors who have put up with years and years of "Little Mary Ellen" and the interesting things that come along with her.

Table Of Contents

Please note, index is included but does not feature page numbers. For electronic versions of this book, the index may be used primarily as a guide for searching key words.

Foreword from the American Society for the Prevention of Cruelty to Animals
(Stephen S. Zawistowski)

It is a most unlikely story. A man with neither pets nor children embarks on a crusade that will forever change the way we view and treat the most vulnerable members of our households and communities. Henry Bergh was a man who had it made. He was wealthy, well connected and happily married. He and his wife Katherine enjoyed travel, the arts and soirees with the social elite. Bergh did not fit the mold of the evolving American hero as common man rising to uncommon needs as did his contemporary, Abraham Lincoln. Rather, he hearkened back to a different sort of hero called to action by a sense of *noblesse oblige*, men of stature and prominence, risking prestige and fortune to defend the defenseless and preserve an ideal.

It is a story with biblical allusions. Bergh's life as a dilettante is divided from his legend and accomplishment by an epiphany. It is said that when riding through St. Petersburgh Russia while serving in the American embassy, Bergh stops his carriage to prevent the beating of a horse by a Russian peasant. Saul of Damascus was stricken from his horse by a bolt of lightening and arose as Paul to preach the gospel. Bergh would emerge from his own epiphany to become an avenging angel protecting

6

animals and children; an image memorialized in the ASPCA seal by Frank Leslie. When Bergh rescues little Mary Ellen from her hellish existence, it is hard not to see the shadow of Jesus raising the daughter of Jarius. Bergh brought Mary Ellen back to the land of the living and to light and her growth and maturation as a loving and caring mother are surely signs of rebirth in a new life.

It is a story of intrigue, politics, betrayal and triumph. Bergh begins the work of the ASPCA with the help of his influential friends. They cheer his efforts to stop teamsters beating their horses, butchers stacking live calves like so much cordwood and the riff raff who gather at Kit Burn's fighting pit for blood sports. However, when he meddles with their profits by stopping trolleys overloaded with passengers to spare the horses, or spoils their gentile sport by attacking foxhunts and pigeon shoots, they work to limit the power and influence of Bergh and the ASPCA. Bergh is stalwart against their efforts and his final victory is ensured as cities across the nation fan the sparks of his passion and form SPCAs to carry his vision from one end of the continent to the other.

It is a story of sweeping grandeur and compelling simplicity. Kindness can triumph over cruelty.

It is a story for our time. As we struggle with the complex questions of hatred and violence that shatter our world, it is good to know that compassion can cross barriers. Henry Bergh showed us that it was possible to cross the barriers of species to understand and prevent cruelty. Surely, it must be possible to cross the less significant barriers of race, religion and politics.

It is a story that everyone should know, and I am thankful that Eric and Stephen have brought it, "*Out of the Darkness.*"

Foreword from the New York Society for the Prevention of Cruelty to Children
(Elbridge T. Gerry III and Elbridge T. Gerry Jr., *with* Joseph Gleason)

When Elbridge T. Gerry, our ancestor and namesake, graduated with a law degree from Columbia University, at the age of 22 in 1859, he did not foresee that he would devote his life to one of the most revolutionary movements in the history of humankind, nor that he would become the principal author of the very first chapter of children's rights. The United States of America, of which his own grandfather and namesake was a revolutionary patriot, Founding Father and Vice President, had not even spanned four generations, yet was on the brink of being broken by the issue of states rights, exacerbated by the practice of slavery which had threatened the formation of the federal union from the beginning.

The Civil War and the events immediately surrounding it dramatically altered the composition of our young country. A land of self-sufficient farms, great plantations, and individual shopkeepers, merchants and tradesmen was rapidly transformed by the confluence of an industrial revolution, war production, and a massive, unprecedented wave of immigration into an urban nation characterized by a burst of inventiveness, expansion and creativity, which, coupled with poverty and exploitation, completely overwhelmed the social infrastructure.

Not surprisingly, the postwar period was marked by a spontaneous groundswell of social reform movements, initiated and supported by women and men from all economic and social classes, sustained by private organizations and by enabling legislation. In the climate of this counter-reaction to an outlook in which natural resources, animals and even humans were perceived as objects for exploitation, our ancestor's religiously formed social conscience found an outlet. And so it was that within six years of its founding, Elbridge Gerry, a 33 year old attorney of wealth and privilege, was donating his time, talent and treasure to the cause of preventing animal cruelty as legal counsel to the ASPCA.

The irony that an organization existed to protect animals from cruelty and exploitation but not children, was lost on no one, least of all the press, which immediately began to call for one. The same sentiments that stirred Bergh and Gerry to concern for animals extended to humanity's most vulnerable manifestation, its children, and it was not long before the two men found themselves involved in several cases of child cruelty. Following the successful rescue of Mary Ellen in 1874, it became clear that something for the protection of children was required along the lines of the ASPCA model. When no one came forward, they undertook to organize a Society for the Prevention of Cruelty to Children themselves, expecting that others would step in and give it a life of its own while they focused their efforts on behalf of animals. With Gerry as his chief counsel, Bergh did in fact continue to guide and direct the ASPCA until his death in 1888, also remaining an active member of the New York SPCC's board of directors.

NYSPCC co-founder Elbridge T. Gerry so concentrated his efforts and devoted his life to child protection that the Society was often referred to as "the Gerry Society". During fifty-two years as a member, (forty-nine as a director, forty-five as legal counsel and twenty as president), he authored almost all child protection legislation, prosecuted on behalf of children in the courts and frequently endured the hostility and ridicule of the press, serving all the while without compensation. He not only led the world's first organized child protection agency and facilitated its replication throughout the nation and around the world, he also undertook to bring about a social revolution. When he began this great work for humanity with Bergh and John C. Wright and others, child cruelty and exploitation were generally socially acceptable and in some quarters deemed a virtue. A century and a quarter later, this is no longer the case!

Elbridge Gerry's methods and personality were not those of a Father Flannagan or of Gerry's equally deserving but less widely known friend and contemporary, Father Drumgoole, nor was he a "hands on" street activist like Bergh   His forte was law, organization and administration, and such was his skill, dedication and tenacity in the defense of the young, that on his death he was called "the best friend the children of New York ever had." Elbridge Gerry promoted a concept that was revolutionary, embodied it in our laws and organized and led an agency that continues to pioneer in the prevention of child cruelty, setting thereby "a shining example" to those whose means and ability enable them to take the responsibilities of leadership in movements for the general good.' A man who "might in the springtime of his life have devoted to social activities the prestige of a noted name and the advantages of inherited wealth," he "chose to busy himself in public work that made him for a time the butt of ridicule and …and of hatred to many of his fellow-citizens", giving himself "unsparingly to prevent the unnecessary misery of the child and the dumb animal."

Elbridge Gerry gave even more. He left a living legacy of family commitment to the prevention of child abuse and neglect that has continued to this very day. No less than six of his direct descendants and the spouses of three others have served on the Society's board of directors, a contribution of almost two centuries of uncompensated service, service not lacking in controversy, criticism, public embarrassment and vilification.   Our motivation is the same now as then: the religious insight that each person is of infinite worth before God and that it is especially our duty to protect, nurture and cherish those most vulnerable – our children.   For the four members of the Gerry family currently sitting on the NYSPCC Board of Directors, the story of Mary Ellen is not a way of looking backward, but forward, not a basis for self-congratulation, but an inspiration and a challenge for the future. We welcome the publication of the story of Mary Ellen and of this source book as a catalyst for the Society as it strives to lead the way in writing the second chapter of children's rights, the prevention and eradication of child cruelty and exploitation by the alleviation and elimination of their root causes and by supporting and strengthening families.

The undersigned desire to express their deepest gratitude to Joseph T. Gleason for his invaluable assistance in the preparation of this forward. Joseph Gleason has been employed in the service of the NYSPCC for twenty-eight years and has served as the archivist since 1989.

Elbridge T. Gerry Jr.
Elbridge T. Gerry III

Elbridge T. Gerry Jr., a great grandson and namesake of the SPCC co-founder, is a Director of the Society for forty-three years and its immediate past president, having served in that

11

capacity an unprecedented thirty years and seven months. He succeeded the twenty-five year presidency of his father, who gave sixty-four years as a director of the Society.

Elbridge T. Gerry III, a great, great grandson of the co-founder and Treasurer of the Society has been a member of the board of directors since 1981.

Introduction

"My name is Mary Ellen McCormack. I don't know how old I am; My mother and father are both dead; I have no recollection of a time when I did not live with the Connollys; I call Mrs. Connolly mama; I have never had but one pair of shoes, but can't recollect when that was. I have had no shoes or stockings on this winter; I have never been allowed to go out of the rooms where the Connollys live except in the nighttime, and then only in the yard; I have never had on a particle of flannel. My bed at night is only a piece of carpet, stretched on the floor underneath a window, and I sleep in my little undergarment, with a quilt over me. I am never allowed to play with any children or have any company whatever. Mama has been in the habit of whipping and beating me almost every day. She used to whip me with a twisted whip, a raw hide. The whip always left black and blue marks on my body. I have now on my head two black and blue marks which were made by mama with the whip, and a cut on the left side of my forehead which was made by a pair of scissors in mama's hand. She struck me with the scissors and cut me. I have no recollection of ever having been kissed, and have never been kissed by mama. I have never been taken on my Mama's lap, or caressed or petted. I never dared to speak to anybody, because if I did I would get whipped; I never had, to my recollection, any more clothing than I have on at present, a calico dress and skirt; I have seen stockings and other clothes in our room, but I am not allowed to put them on; whenever mama went out I was locked up in the bedroom; the scissors with which mama struck me are those now shown by Mr. Evans; I don't know for what I was whipped; mama never said anything to me when she whipped me; I do not want to go back to live with mama, because she beats me so; I have no recollection of ever being in the street in my life."

On April 9th, 1874, a severely abused nine-year-old child named Mary Ellen Wilson was rescued from her terrible situation after enduring it for most of her life. Her widely publicized case triggered a nationwide awareness of child abuse, and subsequently, the recognition that children, as well as adults, are entitled to kind treatment.

Now consider that the man who set her rescue in motion was the founder and president of the American Society for the Prevention of Cruelty to Animals (ASPCA), Henry Bergh. Oddly enough, this man's work and many fine achievements, just as this case, has almost been completely buried among the dusty annals of history. On simple analysis, it's not too surprising. Bergh, for a time, co-existed with the likes of Abraham Lincoln, Charles Darwin, Horace Greeley, Henry Ford and P.T. Barnum, to name a few. With these amazing men doing (or poised to do) such amazing things, it's somewhat understandable that Henry Bergh might go relatively unnoticed.

There is good reason this book spends so much time refreshing its readers on the life of Henry Bergh; his kind can not be found on every street corner, and in fact, are more than rare. Only a handful of people today are willing to be laughed at, prodded at, ridiculed, and even attacked – and still go forth and do what they feel is right. Thank goodness for Bergh's unwillingness to fold under pressure of press and popular opinion. His diligence changed the world, as you will undoubtedly take note of in the , 1879 article from Scribner's Weekly, *Henry Bergh and His Work.*

Bergh's inventions were mostly designed for the humane treatment of animals. For instance, he was directly responsible for the invention of the clay pigeon, replacing the unfortunate live pigeons that were once maimed or blinded to make them fly erratically. Bergh's ASPCA also built the first ambulance for horses a full six years before Bellevue Hospital in New York created one for humans.

But in April of 1874, Bergh and his attorney, Elbridge T. Gerry, intervened on behalf of an abused little girl. Their actions shaped the laws protecting children today.

Here is a report written by a man named Jacob Riis. Born in Ribe, Denmark on May 3rd49, the third of fifteen children, he emigrated to the United States in 1870. Working menial jobs to get by day-to-day, he was eventually hired by a news bureau in New York. In 1874, he was offered a job with the *South Brooklyn News*. By 1877, he would work for the *New York Tribune* as a police reporter. During his life, however, Riis did everything possible to shed light on the poor and destitute souls living in New York. He wrote several books, the most popular of which were, 1890's *How the Other Half Lives,* and in 1892, *Children of the Poor*. Both of these volumes

15

consisted largely of photographs revealing the side of New York many of the wealthy did not wish to see. Riis' work was largely responsible for the elimination seedy lodging houses and of the filthy, overcrowded, crime-ridden tenements of Mulberry Bend. "The Bend" is now Columbus Park. Riis was in court the day Mary Ellen Wilson was carried in. In Riis' words:

"I was in a court-room full of men with pale, stern looks. I saw a child brought in, carried in a horse blanket, at the sight of which men wept aloud. I saw it laid at the feet of the judge, who turned his face away; and in the stillness of that court-room, I heard a voice raised, claiming for that child the protection that men had denied it, in the name of the homeless cur of the streets. And I heard the story of little Mary Ellen told again, that stirred the soul of a city, and roused the conscience of a world that had forgotten. The sweet-faced missionary who found Mary Ellen was the wife of a newspaper man – happy augury, where the gospel of faith and gospel of facts join hands, the world moves. She told how the poor consumptive in the dark tenement, at whose bedside she daily read the Bible, could not die in peace while "the child they called Mary Ellen" was beaten and tortured in the next flat; and how on weary feet she went from door to door of the powerful, vainly begging mercy for it and peace for her dying friend . . .

The charitable said, "It is dangerous to interfere between parent and child. Better let it alone"; and the judges said it was even so. It was for them to see that men walked in the way laid down, not to find it – until her woman's heart rebelled against it all, and she sought the great friend of dumb brutes, who made a way.

"The child is an animal," he said. "If there is no justice for it as a human being, it shall at least have the rights of the cur in the street. It shall not be abused."

And as I looked, I knew I was where the first chapter of children's rights was being written under warrant of that made for the dog; for from that dingy court-room whence a wicked woman sent to jail thirty years ago came forth the New York Society for the Prevention of Cruelty to Children, with all it has meant to the world's life. It is quickening its pulse in this day in lands and among peoples who never spoke the name of my city or Mary Ellen's."

Most social workers, Guardian Ad Litem administrators and CASA (Court-Appointed Special Advocates) staff know about Mary Ellen Wilson. Most others outside the field of child protection do not. It is our goal, as the authors of this book, that everyone know of Etta Wheeler's dedication to a single child's welfare, Elbridge T. Gerry's selfless, charitable contribution of his time, Henry Bergh's lifelong dedication to the helpless, and perhaps most importantly, of Mary Ellen Wilson's life, and what her rescue meant to millions of abused children to follow. And while she survived a horrific period of abuse, Mary Ellen did not allow the cycle to repeat itself. She had two daughters and adopted a third, providing a loving home filled with all the things of which she was deprived.

This compilation of documents and information is long overdue for many reasons. It contains every relevant contemporaneous and contemporary newspaper article, photograph, letter, brief communication, and even sheet music for two songs written about Mary Ellen. And perhaps most importantly, this book contains the court transcripts that have been held exclusively in the private records of the New York Society for the Prevention of Cruelty to Children (NYSPCC) for the last 128 years. While these transcripts fall under the category of public record, the New York Municipal Archives can no longer locate the original or a copy thereof. Over the years, fire and several changes in location have either destroyed or buried them forever. After the 1874 trial, the NYSPCC placed a copy of these transcripts in Mary Ellen's file, and once there, it became confidential. They maintained this confidentiality for well over a century.

During this period, many researchers tried unsuccessfully to gain access to the transcripts, but for these reasons of confidentiality, the NYSPCC would not release them without family authorization. Thanks to the cooperation of Mary Ellen's family – namely, her granddaughter, Shirley Mehlenbacher – and the SPCC, we are able to bring them to light in this volume for the first time ever.

****

1

Mary Ellen Wilson: America's First Abused Child

The story of "Little Mary Ellen", the abused child whose rescue by Henry Bergh, founder and president of the American Society for the Prevention of Cruelty to Animals (ASPCA), provided hope for millions of abused and neglected children who followed in her painful footsteps.

Clearly, Mary Ellen was not the first child to experience abuse. However, she was the first abused child whose situation drew national and worldwide attention – both of the press and the public – to the social issue of child abuse.

The famous "My name is Mary Ellen . . ." statement was given by Mary Ellen Wilson in the private chambers of Judge Abraham Lawrence on April 9th, 1874. While most documents provide it as one long soliloquy, the answers were more likely given in response to questions asked by New York Supreme Court Judge Abraham Lawrence, Henry Bergh, and ASPCA attorney, Elbridge T. Gerry in Judge Lawrence's chambers.

The most well-known part of "Little Mary Ellen's" story began in December of 1873, when Marietta "Etta"

Angell Wheeler, wife of Charles and missionary for St. Luke's Mission in New York City, learned about a little abused child living in a tenement building in the city. Wheeler, in her mid-forties at the time, dedicated her daily attentions to the disadvantaged inhabitants of the tenement slums.

Margaret Bingham, the landlord of the building at 325 W 41st Street, where the child and her family lived, reported the situation to Wheeler with the hope that the dedicated missionary might do something to rescue the child from the situation.

Upon hearing the story of the child's abuse, Wheeler was concerned. Through tireless investigation and – and by her own admission – "snooping", she learned as much as she could about the little girl. The child was small, believed to be 5 or 6 years old. Though she was rarely seen by neighbors in the tenement building in which she lived, her screams and footsteps as she ran back and forth to escape her beatings were heard clearly by others through the thin, partition walls. Here are Etta Wheeler's own words regarding the case, published in an October13 publication distributed by the American Humane Association:

The Story of Mary Ellen:
The Beginnings of a Worldwide Child-Saving Crusade

By Mrs. Etta Angell Wheeler, the humanitarian who first discovered and reported the case.

The sufferings of this little girl caused the New York Society for the Prevention of Cruelty to Children, the first of organization of its kind, to be founded in 1874, through the efforts of Henry Bergh, Eldridge T. Gerry, and John D. Wright.

Late in the year 1873, there was brought to me by a poor working woman, the story of a child whose sad case inspired the founding of the first "Society for the Prevention of Cruelty to Children". The woman was a quiet, reserved Scotch woman, truthful and careful of her words. The story was that during the two previous years, there had lived in the rear tenement9 West 41st Street, a family of three persons, a man, a woman and a little girl, supposed to be five or six years old; that during these two years the child had been a close prisoner having been seen only once by the other tenants; and she was often cruelly whipped and very frequently left alone the entire day with the windows darkened, and she was locked in an inner room; that the other occupants of the house had no known to whom to make complaint, the owner of the house, who lived on the premises, refusing to listen.

A week before, the family had moved to the rear tenement 341, the same street. Later in the day, I went to 349 and heard a like story from others; then, hoping to see the child, I went to 341. The house was separated from the one in front by a narrow, paved court; each of the three floors had two apartments, a living room, and a bedroom in each. The living rooms were separated by a thin partition through which, during weeks to come, the cries of the child gave evidence of her unhappy life. The family I sought was on the top floor. Wondering what reason I could give for my intrusion, I knocked at the door. It was not opened. Wishing, if possible, to learn if the child was there, I knocked at the door of the adjoining apartment. A faint voice bade me "Herein." I saw a tidy room, and in the dark bedroom a young German woman apparently very ill.

Next Page: Mary Ellen Wilson on April 9th, 1874. (Courtesy of the George Sim Johnston archives of the NYSPCC.)

While sitting by her bed for a short time she told me of coming with her young husband, not long before, to this land of strangers and strange speech; of her homesickness and failing health. I asked her of her new neighbors. She had not seen them, but there was a child – she had heard it crying – perhaps it too was sick. Promising to come again, I returned to the other apartment where, after a time, the door was slightly opened and a woman's sharp voice asked my errand. I began telling her of her sick and lonely neighbor and talked on until, unconsciously, she had opened the door, so that I could step in. This I did, and being an unbidden guest, made a very brief call. I was there only long enough to see the child and gain my own impression of her condition. While still talking with the woman, I saw a pale, thin child, barefoot; in a thin, scanty dress so tattered that I could see she wore but one garment besides.

It was December and the weather bitterly cold. She was a tiny mite, the size of five years, though as afterward appeared, she was then nine. From a pan set upon a low stool, she stood washing dishes, struggling with a frying pan about as heavy as herself. Across the table lay a brutal whip of twisted leather strands, and the child's meager arms and legs bore many marks of its use. But the saddest part of her story was written on her face in its look of suppression and misery, the face of a child unloved, of a child that had seen only the fearsome side of life. These things I saw while seeming not to see, and I left without speaking to, or of, the child. I never saw her again until the day of her rescue, three months later, but I went away determined, with the help of kind Providence, to rescue her from her miserable life.

How was this to be done? The man worked but irregularly. The woman earned no money. Their dress and living showed very little means. The postman had told the person who brought the first report to me that he left no mail for the family except, frequently, registered letters. Thinking this might mean money for keeping the child, I feared to arouse any suspicion lest the family should disappear, so I determined that no rescue should be attempted until there was a fair prospect of success. I asked advice. No one could tell me what to do.

Marietta "Etta" Angell Wheeler
(Courtesy of the George Sim Johnston
Archives of the NYSPCC)

There seemed no place of appeal. Meanwhile, it was, from the sick woman I was to learn more and more of the cruel treatment now against the thin wall separating the two living rooms; she could but hear much of the abusive treatment. As often as I went to see her, there was a piteous story to hear. At last she was told what had first brought me to the house, and we waited and hoped together.

Weeks went by. Easter Sunday came, bright with sunshine, warm with the breath of spring. As I went into church, passing from the brightness without to the beauty of palms and lilies and organ strains within, the thought of the dying woman and the poor child smote upon me. I was very early and with a few flowers from the altar steps I turned away and went to spend the morning in the tenement. The child had been locked up early in the dark bedroom, the Easter sunshine shut out; the man and woman had gone, and would not return until night. The poor invalid gave the flowers a pathetic welcome and as I sat by her side she told me of Easter Sundays of her childhood in the beloved Rhineland, all homesickness for which had now passed into longing for the land where sickness is not. Yet always she had wished to stay until her little fellow sufferer was rescued. We spoke of Christ, of the Resurrection, of the glorious meaning of Easter Day, and we talked of the child alone in the darkness, and prayed for her release. Poor suffering woman! She knew death stood at the door, and did not yet know he was not to enter until the child she had so pitied was free, and that, in that very Easter week.

I had more than once been tempted to apply to the Society for the Prevention of Cruelty to Animals, but had lacked courage to do what seemed absurd. However, when on the following Tuesday, a niece said: "You are so troubled over that abused child, why not go to Mr. Bergh? She is a little animal, surely." I said at once, "I will go." Within an hour I was at the society's rooms. Mr. Bergh was in his office and listened to my recital most courteously but with a slight air of amusement that such an appeal should be made there. In the end he said: "The case interests me much, but very definite testimony is necessary to warrant interference between a child and those claiming guardianship. Will you not send me a written statement that, at my leisure, I may judge the weight of the evidence and may also have time to consider if this society should interfere? I promise to consider the case carefully."

Mary Ellen Wilson, one year after rescue. (Courtesy of the George Sim Johnston Archives of the NYSPCC.)

It was the first promise of help and I was glad. The next morning I sent a paper giving what I had seen and heard, which was little, and the much that had been told me by others, and what seemed to me their credibility as witnesses.

Going later in the day to see the sick woman, I found in her room a young man with a large official looking book under his arm. Hearing a nurse speak my name as I entered, he said to me: "I was sent to take the census in this house. I have been in every room." I inferred at once that this was a detective for Mr. Bergh. When I left the house, the young man was waiting on the sidewalk to tell me he had seen the child and was then going to Mr. Bergh with his report of her pitiable condition.

The next morning, Thursday, Mr. Bergh called upon me to ask if I would go to the court house, the child having been already sent for. He expressed pleasure that he need not ask me to go to a police court, Judge Lawrence of the Supreme Court having kindly taken the case. After we had waited a long time in the judge's court, two officers came in, one of whom had the little girl in his arms. She was wrapped in a carriage blanket, and was without other clothing other than the two ragged garments I had seen her in months before. Her body was bruised, her face disfigured, and the woman, as if to make testimony sure against herself, had the day before, struck the child with a pair of shears, cutting a gash through the left eyebrow and down the cheek, fortunately escaping the eye.

The child was sobbing bitterly when brought in, but there was a touch of the ludicrous with it all. While one of the officers had held the infuriated woman, the other had taken away the terrified child. She was still shrieking as they drove away and they called a halt at the first candy

27

shop, so that she came into the court weeping, but waving as a weapon of defense a huge stick of peppermint candy. Poor child! It was her one earthly possession. The investigation proceeded. The child's appearance was testimony enough, little of mine was needed, and thus, on Thursday, April 9th, 1874, her rescue was accomplished.

This Mr. Bergh had effected within forty-eight hours after first hearing of the case. The next day, the woman, who had so often forgotten her own suffering in pity for the child, died, happy that little Mary Ellen was free. Now, fir the first time, we knew the child's name.

The prosecution of the woman who had so ill-treated her followed soon. One witness was a representative of the institution from which the woman had taken the child, then less than two years old. No inquiry as to the child's welfare had been made by the institution during the intervening seven years. Record of her admission to this institution had been lost in a fire. The testimony of fellow tenants, and the damaging witness of the woman against herself, under cross-examination, secured her conviction and she was sentenced to the penitentiary for a year. When leaving the court house I tried to thank Mr. Bergh for the rescue of the child, and asked if there could not now be a Society for the Prevention of Cruelty to Children, which should do for abused children what was being so well done for animals? He took my hand and said very emphatically: "There shall be one." Today all the world knows how well that promise was kept. The time had come for a forward movement in the welfare of children and little Mary Ellen's hand had struck the hour.

The child was rescued – what was to be done with her? The press had given the case wide publicity, reports had drawn fanciful pictures of her beauty and attractiveness so that from every quarter from the West to

Florida, and from England, came offers of adoption. The neglected, hindered child would require painstaking patience, and those uncertain offers were declined. Some attempts to obtain her through fictitious claims of relationship were investigated by Judge Lawrence and proved fictitious. After a short time she was put in a home, not one for young children, but for grown girls, some of them wayward, who were being trained for service.

To me this was most unsatisfactory and after waiting some months, I expressed my disapproval to Judge Lawrence who was now her guardian. He consulted with Mr. Bergh and soon put Mary Ellen at my disposal. I took her to my mother near Rochester, NY, whose heart and home were always open to the needy.

Here began a new life. The child was an interesting study, so long shut within four walls and now in a new world. Woods, fields, green things growing, were all strange to her. She had not known them. She had to learn, as a baby does, to walk upon the ground – she had walked only upon floors and her eye told her nothing of uneven surfaces. She was wholly untaught. She knew nothing of right and wrong except as related to punishments; did not know of the Heavenly Father; had had no companionship with children or toys. But in this home there were other children, and they taught her as children alone can teach each other. They taught her to play, to be unafraid, to know her rights and to claim them. She shared their happy, busy lives from the making of mud pies up to charming birthday parties, and was fast becoming a normal child.

I had taken her to my mother in June. In the autumn following, my mother died. She had asked that, after her death, my sister living nearby should take Mary Ellen. This she did and under her care were passed years of home and school life, of learning all good household ways; of instruction in church and Sunday school, and in gaining the love and the esteem of all who knew her.

When twenty-four she was married to a worthy man and has proved a good home maker and a devoted wife and mother. To her children, two bright, dutiful daughters, it has been her joy to give a happy childhood in sharp contrast to her own. If the memory of her earliest years is sad, there is this comfort that the cry of her wrongs awoke the world to the need of organized relief for neglected and abused children.

2

Mary Ellen's Family

Mary Ellen's mother, whose maiden name was Frances Connor, came to America from London, England in 1858 at approximately 18 years of age. The reason she left her family in Europe to make her life in America is unknown. Her parents, Michael and Mary Connor, were apparently of limited financial means, and perhaps this contributed to Frances' leaving home. Frances' younger sister, Ellen Connor, who was 10 years old at the time, stayed with her parents in London.

Family letters tell us that Frances Connor, known by her family and friends as "Fanny", accompanied her uncle, John Connor, to New York, though there is no information available to indicate how long they remained together once in America. John Connor Jr., Frances' cousin, also made the journey with them.

Soon after her arrival, Frances began work at the Saint Nicholas Hotel as a laundress, where she made the acquaintance of her husband-to-be, Thomas Wilson.

Wilson has been described in sworn testimony by Fanny's cousin, John Connor Jr., as "an Irishman about 5'7" or 5'8" tall [illegible] and no side whiskers". Wilson also worked at the St. Nicholas, employed as an oyster "opener", or "shucker".

Love and War

Thomas and Fanny were married in 1861, around the onset of the Civil War. Late in the same year, according to John Connor's testimony, Thomas Wilson volunteered to fight for New York's famous Irish Brigade.

After his first tour of duty, also according to Connor's testimony, Thomas Wilson re-enlisted in Hawkins's 2nd Fire Zouaves, possibly enticed by furloughs and bonuses. An entry can be found in Civil War records, showing that in 1861, Private Thomas Wilson years old, was mustered into service with the Zouaves, but this document conflicts with Connor's testimony that Wilson was mustered in with the 69th. The first name Thomas and surname Wilson were both common at the time (and now) so it could have easily been a different Thomas Wilson.

Assuming Wilson did join the "Fighting 69th", he left New York in late 1861, the brigade at nearly full strength with between 800 to 1000 men. By December of 1862 after the battle at Fredericksburg, according to the report below, there were 50 rank and file and two officers remaining, half the strength of a company. According to the commanding captain, James Saunders, the 69th Irish Brigade left the battlefield in 1862, having fought itself into oblivion in twelve months. Here is an excerpt from Saunders' report:

Camp near Falmouth, December 22, 1862

"In Compliance with General Orders received December 21, I herby certify that the Sixty-Ninth

Regiment New York Volunteers entered the battle of Fredericksburg, on December 13, 1862, commanded by Col. Robert Nugent, and 18 commissioned officers and 210 rank and file, in which the above numbered regiment lost 16 commissioned officers and 160 rank and file, leaving Capt. James Saunders, Lieutenant Milliken, and Lieutenant L. Brennan to bring the remnant of the regiment off the battle-field.

James Saunders, Captain,
Comdg. Sixty-Ninth Regt. NY Vols

The exact date of Mary Ellen's birth is not known, but John Connor's testimony states:

"I met Fanny on Spring Street about this time [1863] with a child in her arms about three weeks old. She called it by name Mary Ellen and said she had named it after her mother, Mary Connor, and her sister Ellen Connor, now Ellen Fitzgerald. The child had whitish hair. I stood talking to my cousin Fanny for about half an hour. This was about 1863."

Other research has placed Mary Ellen's birth date around March of 1864, but John Connor's estimation of "about 1863" does not contradict this enough to warrant further research.

While Wilson may have been aware of Mary Ellen's birth through letters from Fanny, he probably never met his daughter. Thomas Wilson was killed either in Spotsylvania, Virginia or Cold Harbor, Virginia around May of 1864.

Following the death of her husband, Frances Wilson drew two dollars per week as a soldier's widow, but this amount must have been insufficient for her to survive and care for Mary Ellen. She soon returned to work at the St. Nicholas Hotel, once again as a laundress. She eventually placed Mary Ellen in the care of Mary Score, a woman living in the tenement houses on Mulberry Street. The area, known as "The Bend" or "Mulberry Bend", after the elbow-shaped turn in the middle of the street, was renowned for its hoodlums, poverty and overcrowded, unsanitary conditions.

Baby Farming

Though Mary Score has been referred to as a "baby farmer" in some books and articles, the actual practice of baby farming involved babies being "murdered" for their monetary value. Unwanted children of poor women were placed in the "care" of someone else (usually another woman). The mother would pay the baby farmer a fee to take the baby off her hands. The younger babies were better for the farmers, as their deaths were easier to pass off as "accidental". This practice was very common in England in the 18th and 19th centuries, but immigration inevitably made the practice more common in America.

There is no evidence or indication that Fanny intended that Mary Ellen die in the care of Mary Score. Indeed, Score later testified in court that Fanny returned on a semi-regular basis to see Mary Ellen, and even held and kissed her. A traditional baby farmer probably would not have turned the child over to the Department of Charities and Corrections, as Score eventually did Mary Ellen.

Following page: The imfamous Mulberry Bend, circa 1880. (From How the Other Half Lives, Jacob Riis, 1890.)

John Connor's testimony further states that he ran into Fanny Wilson again in 1865, and she told him "she had put out the child to nurse with a woman, who said the child had died." Score, who testified in court, was never asked about this directly, and never mentioned it. She simply stated that the soldier's relief ticket was "kept where payment was given," and that she could not afford to keep the child. Her testimony and official documents show that on July 7th, 1865, Score placed Mary Ellen with the Department of Public Charities and Corrections under the direction of the Superintendent of the Outdoor Poor, George Kellock.

Three days later, on July 10th, 1865, Mary Ellen Wilson was placed in an alms house located on Blackwell's Island.

Mary Ellen on Blackwell's Island

Blackwell's Island (now Roosevelt Island) was acquired by New York City in 1828 for $30,000.00, and was eventually home to all of the following institutions:

Small Pox Hospital
Charity Hospital
Penitentiary
Alms Houses
Hospital for Incurables
Prisoner Workhouse
Lunatic Asylum

The alms house became Mary Ellen's new home. Though historical descriptions of the alms house indicate it was primarily used to house adult men and women, this is where Mary Ellen was placed, and where she remained for the next six months. Mary Ellen was one of the fortunate survivors of New York orphanages, which experienced
average death rates of 85% during this period of rampant disease and unsanitary conditions. Despite statistics and an infant's vulnerability to disease, Mary Ellen survived her time there.

But Mary Ellen's life was about to change dramatically. A married couple, Thomas and Mary McCormick, arrived at the Blackwell's Island alms house and paid a visit to George Kellock. Thomas, a butcher by trade, then chose Mary Ellen as his own daughter, saying that he had had an affair with a "no good woman" who had left the child there.

On January 2nd, 1866, with no proof other than Thomas McCormick's word and a letter from the

McCormick's family doctor saying the couple was fit to take care of a child, Mary Ellen was turned over by the Department of Public Charities and Corrections to Thomas and Mary McCormick, to remain in their custody until her 18th birthday.

Since it is unlikely that evidence will ever be obtained to confirm McCormick's claim of paternity, there can be only speculation. If he was telling the truth, was the woman with whom he had the affair Frances Wilson? If McCormick was lying, why choose this particular female child, at such a young age that she could not yet help with tasks around the house?

Strangely enough, these authors have never heard or read about anyone asking these questions before. The assumption seemed to be made that Mary Ellen was Thomas Wilson's child.

But in court testimony, Mary McCormick herself (Mary Connolly, during testimony) acknowledged that her husband might have had an affair with Fanny Wilson, though she never met Wilson or had any direct evidence of it. Since research (to date) has not produced furlough records for Thomas Wilson, he also cannot be placed in New York City on a date that would support the time frame of Fanny Connor's pregnancy or Mary Ellen's subsequent birth.

It is known that Thomas and Mary McCormick once had three children of their own, all having died prior to their adoption of Mary Ellen. We also know from the same sworn testimony that they had two girls and one boy, but we do not know exactly when they were born, when they died, or what caused their deaths.

The McCormicks took Mary Ellen away from Blackwell's Island on the 2nd of January, when Mary Ellen was approximately two years old, but no paperwork at all was signed the day they took her home.

This was a legal and ethical point to be raised later by officials investigating the rightful custody of Mary Ellen. The McCormicks returned to Kellock's offices on January 15th to sign the proper papers, making their indenture of Mary Ellen official.

Thomas McCormick died in August of that year, seven months after Mary Ellen came into their charge. Following is the official indenture as it was recorded on January 15th, 1866:

> This indenture witnesseth: that Mary Ellen Wilson, aged one year and six months hath put herself and by these presents and with the consent and approbation of the Commissioners of Public Charities and Correction of the City of New York doth voluntarily and of her own free will and accord put herself to adopt to Thomas McCormick, butcher, and Mary his wife, residing at 866 Third Avenue in the City of New York, and after the manner of an adopted child to serve from the day of the date hereof for and during the full end and term of sixteen years and six months next ensuing. During all of which time the said child her parent faithfully shall serve, his secrets keep, his lawful commands everywhere readily obey; she shall do no damage to her said parents nor see it done by others without preventing the same so far as she lawfully may, and give notice thereof to her said parent; she shall not waste her said master's goods nor lend unlawfully to any; she shall not absent herself day nor night from her said parent's service without his leave nor frequent ale houses, taverns, not play houses and in all things behave herself as a faithful child ought to during the said term; and the said

parent shall use the utmost of his endeavor to teach or cause to be taught or instructed the said child in the trade and mystery of housekeeping and plain sewing, and procure and provide for her sufficient meat, drink, apparel, mending, lodging and washing fitting for an adopted child and cause her to be instructed in reading, writing, and arithmetic during the said term; and at the expiration thereof shall give a new Bible to the said child and a suit of new clothing in addition to her old ones in wear, and shall furnish to her at all times when necessary or proper medical assistance and attendance and nursing, and at all proper times the utensils and articles required for keeping her healthy and cleanly.

Special. To report to the said Commissioners of Public Charities and Correction once in each year the character and condition of said girl. And for the due performance of all and singular the covenants and agreements aforesaid the said parties bind themselves unto each other firmly by these presents.

In witness whereof the said parties have interchangeably set their hands and seal hereunto. Dated the Thirteenth day of February in the ninetieth year of the Independence of the United States of America and in the year of our Lord 1866.

> Signed and delivered
> Thomas McCormick (Seal)
> In the presence of
> Mary McCormick   (Seal)

H.W. Boswell   George Kellock (Seal)
    Superintendent O.D.P. (Out Door Poor)
    For Mary Ellen Wilson

On the back of the paper is the following endorsement.

New York, Feb 15, 1866

We consent to and approve of the within indenture providing all the requirements are complied with. On behalf of the Board of Commissioners of Public Charities and Correction.

Attest.   James Bowen   Isaac Bell
           Secretary   President

The Abusive Years

After her husband died of Cholera in August of 1866, Mary McCormick remarried to a man named Francis Connolly, thus becoming Mary Connolly. According to Mary Connolly's testimony, this occurred in August or September of 1867.

Mary Ellen's home life during her infant and toddler years is largely a mystery. Only after Methodist church worker, Etta Wheeler, was told about the child's abusive situation did witnesses step forward and tell what they had seen and heard up to two years prior. Mary Ellen's abuse can be verified by Margaret Bingham's testimony, the landlord of the building where the Connollys lived from September 1871 until December 1873. Unfortunately, with all we do know, the period from 1866 to 1871 remains a six-year wide gap in the historical account of Mary

Ellen's young life. Aside from the fact that Mary Ellen survived, there is no reason to assume her treatment was any more humane in her earlier years.

In the next chapter we take a look at Henry Bergh's ASPCA and his attorney, Elbridge T. Gerry – specifically, their desire to protect helpless animals amid outside pressure to extend this help and protection to the abused and needy children of the city and state of New York.

3

Henry Bergh, Elbridge T. Gerry and the ASPCA

Henry Bergh's Early Life

Henry Bergh (1813-1888) was born on August 29th13 to Christian and Elizabeth Bergh. Christian Bergh III, whose descendants came to America in 1700, was himself a native of New York, and owned a shipyard covering thirty-six lots in Manhattan, at a time when the southern tip of the island harbored only 100,000 inhabitants.

Henry was the youngest of three children. Edwin, his brother, was eleven years older, and his sister Jane was five years his senior.

While Henry occasionally accompanied his father at the shipyard, dressed to resemble a miniature of the elder Bergh, he was not to join in the family business. Instead, as he grew well over six feet tall and began to show a mustache, he took to dancing, music and art. Instead of following in his brother Edwin's academic footsteps and earning his degree, Henry dropped out of Columbia College before his class of '34 graduated.

Edwin Bergh took over the shipyard in 1837 when his father grew too tired to keep it. Henry wanted none of it, attracted instead by the most fashionable New York drawing rooms and opening nights at the theater.

In these early years of fun and frolic, Bergh was often accompanied by Gordon Bennett, whose astounding new penny sheet, the New York Herald, would eventually become a harsh critic of Bergh's later efforts to protect animals.

Early in 1839, a young woman named Catherine Matilda Taylor caught Henry's eye, and the two soon became the talk of the town. Shortly after word spread of their budding romance, Henry and Matilda's wedding was announced for September 10th of the very same year.

But on the morning of the wedding, Henry panicked. He called upon Matilda with a special wish for her to fulfill. With St. Mark's Church filled to the brim with guests anticipating a grand ceremony, they eloped, leaving all to wonder what became of them. This was typical of the Henry Bergh who emerged later, unconcerned with the opinions of others, so long as they did not interfere with his plans.

Young Henry Bergh. (Courtesy of the George Sim Johnston Archives of the NYSPCC.)

In 1843, Henry's father died, and his mother followed three years later. The Bergh children fell heir to a

43

hearty fortune, and Henry and Matilda made use of their portion by extensive travel abroad.

Bergh Finds a Purpose

In a journal entry, written after visiting the *Plaza de Toros* in Seville, Spain, Henry Bergh showed the first sign of what was to become his passion. Much to his dismay, he discovered bullfighting. Here is what he wrote:

"About twenty-five horses and eight bulls were destroyed today, and one of the *picadors* was carried off the field badly hurt. But one's sympathies are not with the men, for they have reason, know their danger, are the inventors of this scene, and therefore richly merit death in any shape. It would doubtless serve the cause of humanity if a score of them were killed, including the governor and Alcalde at each exhibition."

As the years went by, and civil unrest in America grew, Bergh became a staunch supporter of the "free North". In May of 1861, he wrote in a letter to his nephew:

"Whichever side may win, the most essential is, in my opinion, a total change of government, by the destruction of the principle of universal suffrage – the rock upon which our nation is now split, although it seems to be the question of slavery . . . My advice to you, my dear fellow, is to go to work and create a military despotism, until that cursed incubus, universal suffrage, is destroyed; then give to everybody the privileges his talents, virtue and worth entitled him . . . At any rate, let your views differ ever so much from mine in these particulars, I am sure we think alike on one point, and that is, that those infernal Southern traitors and slavers shall be beaten, cost what it will!"

By 1863, Henry was appointed by President Lincoln to fill the shoes of Bayard Taylor as Secretary of the American Legation in St. Petersburg. He arrived in Russia on July 12th to take up his duties under the American Minister, Cassius M. Clay.

One day, as Henry rode in the Legation carriage, he saw a droshky driver beating his horse unmercifully with a whip. As Bergh ordered his driver to stop the carriage, the droshky driver did not even bother to look up. Bergh leaned forward, dressed in his diplomatic lace and gold braids, and told the driver, "Tell that fellow to stop!"

The coachman, using fluent Russian, barked the command. The startled peasant looked up to the gorgeous carriage, threw his whip aside, and began to bow. Bergh ordered his driver onward, satisfied and a bit surprised.

In weeks and months to come, Bergh ordered his driver down alleys and side streets, looking for more cruelties practiced on animals. While the Legation staff was astonished by Bergh's actions, he said, "At last I've found a way to utilize my gold lace – and about the best use that can be made of it."

Bergh had once admitted, "I was never especially interested in animals – though I always had a natural feeling of tenderness for creatures that suffer. What struck me most forcibly was that mankind derived immense benefits from these creatures, and gave them in return not the least protection."

Bergh resigned his post after a little more than a year in service, citing the Russian climate was not suitable to him and Matilda. During his investigation into the protection of animals, Bergh learned that the idea of kindness to animals had already taken root in England.

He traveled to London and met with the Earl of Harrowby, president of England's Royal SPCA. He stayed for several months, and learned all he could learn about the organization.

In June of 1865, Bergh returned to New York with a goal: To create a Society for the Prevention of Cruelty to Animals in America. By April of the following year, he put together enough supporters to achieve that goal. The official charter reads:

"The undersigned, sensible of the cruelties inflicted upon Dumb Animals by thoughtless and inhuman persons, and desirous of suppressing the same – alike from considerations affecting the well being of society, as well as mercy to the brute creation – consent to become patrons of a Society having in view the realization of these objects."

The signers included, among others:

Mayor John T. Hoffman
Peter Cooper
John Jacob Astor, Jr.
Henry Clews & Co.
James Lenox
Alexander T. Stewart
James J. and C.V.S. Roosevelt
John A Dix
A. Oakey Hall

Harper & Brothers
Hamilton Fish
James Gallatin
William C. Bryant
George Bancroft
James W. Gerard
Horace Greeley
James T. Brady
Henry Bergh

After the American Society for the Prevention of Cruelty to Animals got off the ground, a wealthy yachtsman and well-known attorney in the city, Elbridge T. Gerry, came forth to offer his services to Henry Bergh.

The Gerry name was not unknown to Bergh, nor was the Gerry family's illustrious history. The first Elbridge T. Gerry (a merchant shipper) was a signer of the Declaration of Independence. He also held a seat in the Continental Congress in 1776, serving until 1785 when he retired to Cambridge, Massachusetts. Gerry ran and was elected governor of Massachusetts in 1810, and served three years of his term before being elected as James Madison's vice-president in 1813. Elbridge T. Gerry died in office only a year later, survived by his wife, Louisa, three sons and four daughters.

Herny Bergh, ASPCA President.
(Courtesy of the George Sim Johnston Archives of the NYSPCC.)

His grandson, obviously a principal subject of this chapter, "Commodore" Elbridge Thomas Gerry (1837-1927), was a reformer by nature. A yachtsman and attorney, his position as legal advisor to the American

Society for the Prevention of Cruelty to Animals, and the case of Mary Ellen Wilson – and before that, Emily Thompson – led to his founding, with the help of Bergh, the New York Society for the Prevention of Cruelty to Children (NYSPCC, sometimes called the Gerry Society). Gerry devoted most of his life to the cause of helping children, which became a national movement. He and his wife, Louisa M. Gerry had two sons, Peter and Robert, and two daughters, Angelica and Francis.

When Gerry first approached Bergh and offered to represent the ASPCA, Bergh let him know he would not be able to pay him. Gerry didn't mind, and in fact, had never expected payment. He immediately reviewed the many bills Bergh had in mind, prepared them to meet legal standards, and headed to Albany. He was highly respected and a master at his craft, brilliant at pushing Bergh's many animal protection laws through a reluctant legislature.

Because Bergh and Gerry eventually instigated Mary Ellen's rescue, the following chapter will explain how they came to rescue a child, when their specialty was, of course, animals. First, one myth must be quelled:

Mary Ellen was not rescued because she was a "little animal", nor was she rescued by the ASPCA, specifically. She was rescued because Bergh and Gerry recognized she was as helpless and powerless to remedy her own situation as "the cur in the street", and therefore deserved the same protection. The method of her rescue, while innovative and groundbreaking, was not carried out under the laws protecting animals, but under a section of the ancient Habeas corpus Act of 1679. The translation of the Latin term, *Habeas corpus* is literally, "You should have the body."

The particular section of the Act utilized (section 65) states:

> Whenever it shall appear by satisfactory proof
> that anyone is held in illegal confinement or
> custody, and that there is good reason to
> believe that he will be carried out of the state
> or suffer some irreparable injury before he can

be relieved by the issuing of a Habeas corpus or certiorari, any court or officer authorized to issue such writs may issue a warrant under his hand and seal reciting the facts and directed to any sheriff, constable, or other person, and commanding such officer or person to take such prisoner and forthwith to bring him before such court or office to be dealt with according to law.

While this fact may remove some of the mystique and fascination for many, it is still quite amazing what these two compassionate men achieved. Henry Bergh forged ahead for the remaining years of his life, ensuring the growth of his precious ASPCA until his death in 1888. Elbridge T. Gerry took over as president of the New York Society for the Prevention of Cruelty to Children in 1879, and continued to head up the organization until 1901.

Elbridge T. Gerry, ASPCA Attorney. (Courtesy of the George Sim Johnston Archives of the NYSPCC.)

The following article was written in 1879 for Scribner's Magazine. In it, several stories are related, as well as more detail on this caring man's past as well as his effect on the future – with doubtless more to come.

HENRY BERGH AND HIS WORK

It may almost be said of Henry Bergh that he has invented a new type of goodness, since invention is only the perception and application of truths that are eternal. He has certainly laid restraining hands on a fundamental evil, that blind and strangely human passion of cruelty, the taint of barbarism that lingers through ages of refining influences, to vent its cowardly malice on weak humanity and defenseless dumb animals.

Henry Bergh is a stalwart hero, a moral reformer worthy of an enlightened and practical epoch. This is easily said and maintained now that a denial of the beneficence of his work would be accepted by most persons as a confession of moral turpitude; it is here said in simple justice to one who has braved more obloquy in the discharge of an honorable duty than any other man in the community, and carried a worthy cause, through ridicule and abuse, to assured success.

The position Mr. Bergh occupies at the head of one of the greatest moral agencies of the time, is not more unique than his personal character. Here is a man of refined sensibilities and tender feelings, who relinquished an honored position and the enjoyment of wealth, to become the target of sneers and public laughter, for the sake of principles of humanity the most unselfish by day and by night, in sunshine and storm, he gives his strength to the cause as freely as he aided it with his fortune.

For a few years his person and his purposes were objects of ridicule, in the less scrupulous public prints, and on the streets. He was bullied by lawyers

"The Inspiration," written by Henry Bergh and signed by Bergh, Gerry and Wright. (Courtesy of the George Sim Johnston Archives of the NYSPCC.)

in courts of justice, and took his revenge according to Gospel precept. He was called a fanatic, a visionary, a seeker after notoriety, and a follower of Don Quixote. But faith and courage never forsook him, nor the will to shield a dumb animal from a brutal blow and help a fellow human to control his evil passions. The results and his reward are already proportionate to his labors, for the legislatures of thirty-three states have decided that dumb animals have rights that masters must respect; and the Court of Errors, the highest tribunal in the Empire State, has recently confirmed the equity and constitutionality of the cruelty laws.

Thirteen years of devoted labor have wrought no very great change in the appearance and manner of Henry Bergh. If the lines of his careworn face have multiplied, they have also responded to the kindly influence of public sympathy and the release of his genial disposition from austere restraint. A visitor who had no claims on Mr. Bergh's indulgence once remarked, "I was alarmed by the dignity of his presence and disarmed by his politeness."

Since Horace Greeley's death, no figure more familiar to the public has walked the streets of the metropolis. Nature gave him an absolute patent on every feature and manner of his personality. His commanding stature of six feet is magnified by his erect and dignified bearing. A silk hat with straight rim covers with primness the severity of his presence. A dark brown or dark blue frock overcoat encases his broad shoulders and spare, yet sinewy, figure. A decisive hand grasps a cane, strong enough to lean upon, and competent to be a defense without looking like a standing menace. When this cane, or even his finger, is raised in warning, the cruel driver is quick to understand and heed the gesture.

On the crowded street, he walks with a slow, slightly swinging pace peculiar to himself. Apparently preoccupied, he is yet observant of everything about him and mechanically notes the condition from head to hoof of every passing horse. Everybody looks into the long, solemn, finely chiseled and bronzed face wearing an expression of firmness and benevolence. Brown locks fringe a broad and rounded forehead. Eyes between blue and hazel, lighted by intellectual fires, are equally ready to dart authority or show compassion. There is energy of character in a long nose of the purest Greek type; melancholy in a mouth rendered doubly grave by deep lines, thin lips and a sparse, drooping mustache, and determination in a square chin of leonine strength. The head, evenly poised, is set on a stout neck rooted to broad shoulders.

In plainness, gravity, good taste, individuality and unassuming and self-possessed dignity, his personality is a compromise between a Quaker and a French nobleman whose life and thoughts no less than long descent are his title to nobility. Almost every fourth person knows him by sight, and the whisper, "That's Henry Bergh," follows him, like a tardy herald, wherever be goes. Parents stop and point out to their children the man who is kind to the dumb animals. Many enthusiastic men and women address themselves to him, often saying: "You don't know me, Mr. Bergh, but I know you and wish to grasp your hand and tell how much I am in sympathy with your work." He courteously offers his hand and his thanks, says a pleasant word freighted with quiet humor or common sense, for he is a quick and ready conversationalist, and bows himself on his way.

If he sees a disabled or overloaded horse he stops the vehicle and lets his judgment decide whether the lame animal shall be sent to the stable, or the load reduced. Frequently the driver is willing to argue the question, but not so often now as formerly. When he sees an omnibus driver in a passion with his horses, he raises his cane and the alert eye of the Jehu, dropping on a familiar figure, knows at once with whom he has to deal.

Mr. Bergh's town residence is well located on Fifth Avenue (his summer residence being situated on the shores of Lake Mahopac). After the heavy snow storm in January last, as he was taking his customary morning walk down the avenue toward his office, he saw at a cross street on Murray Hill a burly fellow whipping a stout horse, who was yet unable to budge a heavy load of wood, owing to the depth of the snow. Mr. Bergh went to the animal's defense and told the driver to lessen the load by getting down. The latter offered to do as he pleased about that, adding that it wasn't no load at all. Several characters of sympathetic roughness came up and volunteered the opinion that it wasn't no load at all. They made loud remarks, too, about arbitrary action, and the value of a free country.

"Enough," said Mr. Bergh, stepping into the snow; "We'll call it no load at all, but you get down and then we'll see if you won't have to take off half your load." The driver stood up and beat his horse in defiance, and by this time a large crowd was awaiting the result of the conflict. Mr. Bergh stepped to the horse's head and in a moderate tone of voice that wanted no element of authority said: "You get off that load at once or I shall take you off." The driver obeyed and the horse started the load.

"When you came over here," he concluded, addressing himself to the driver's sympathizers, "you thought a free country was a place where you could do whatever you liked. That's a mistaken idea of a free man."

This is one of his curb-stone speeches, often used with effect: "Now, gentlemen, consider that you are American citizens living in a republic. You make your own laws; no despot makes them for you. And I appeal to your sense of justice and your patriotism, oughtn't you to respect what you yourselves have made?"

One winter's day he met two large men comfortably seated on a ton of coal, with one horse straining to drag the cart through the snow. He ordered them to get down, and after an altercation pulled them down. At another time he stood at the southwest corner of Washington Square, inspecting the horses of the Seventh Avenue Railroad. Several weak and lame horses were ordered to be sent to the stables, and a blockade of overloaded cars soon ensued. A loafer on a car platform, annoyed at the delay, began to curse Mr. Bergh, who stood on the curb-stone three feet distant, turning a deaf ear till the spectators began to urge the bully on. Then, losing his patience, he seized the reins and suspended the movement of the car until the order was complied with.

Once, Mr. Bergh ordered a gang of country gas-pipe layers to fill up one-half of a trench they had dug directly across crowded Greenwich Street, even under the railway track.

Moral suasion and a resolute bearing are Henry Bergh's most potent auxiliaries. Only rarely has he been forced to use his muscular strength to defend himself. The man gave a surly refusal which would have caused his arrest had not a stranger stepped out of the crowd and said: "Mike, you better do what that man tells you, for he's the law and the gospel in this city."

"The law and the gospel is it then?" replied Mike, surveying Mr. Bergh from head to foot. "Well, he don't look a bit like it."

55

"No matter, but he is," enforced the stranger, "and if you can take a friend's advice, you will fill up that trench." And the trench was filled.

It is a compliment to Henry Bergh's tact and moderation in the use of his great authority, that he has won the respect of most of the drivers of the city; these people may frequently be seen lifting their hats to him, a courtesy always acknowledged with a bow. Horse-car drivers have been known to leave their cars and run to the assistance of his officers, notably when Superintendent Hartfield was attacked at Madison Square.

About half-past nine or ten o'clock in the morning, the President of the American Society for the Prevention of Cruelty to Animals walks into the general offices at Fourth Avenue and Twenty-second Street. He does not start as every newcomer does at sight of the stuffed Newfoundland dog in the vestibule. In the main business office on the first floor are exhibited instruments of cruelty to animals, of brutal and ingenious patterns, and the effigies of bloody gamecocks and bull-dogs, and photographs of pitiable horses, a perfect chamber of horrors. On the second floor is Mr. Bergh's office, a light and cheerful room comfortably furnished, in which his letters are written and received.

On the day of the writer's visit, a check for $100 was received from a lady. Many such letters are received from women, who sympathize most warmly in the work of Mr. Bergh's society. "Yes," he adds in reply to a question, "I suppose it is a mark of confidence in me. If I were dependent upon the society for a salary it might be different. The chief obstacle to success of movements like this is that they almost invariably gravitate into questions of money or politics. Such questions are repudiated here completely."

"There is no sum of money or public position that I could take. If I were paid a large salary, or perhaps any salary, I should lose that enthusiasm which has been my strength and my safeguard."

"I dread to visit those butchers," said Mr. Bergh one morning, "and have postponed going till it amounts to criminal neglect. Three-fourths of the butchers of the city are Hebrews. Their religion obliges them to bleed to death the animals they slaughter. So they hook a chain around the hind leg of a bullock, jerk up the struggling beast, head downward, and cut his throat. Well, their religion doesn't require them to suspend an animal by the hind leg, which frequently dislocates the hip and lacerates the flesh. This brutal and shocking torture must be stopped."

Among the letters to be answered are those calling for suggestions for founding similar societies, and this class of correspondence has come from South America or remoter parts of the globe. Recently Mr. Bergh drafted a bill of cruelty laws to be presented to the legislature of Arkansas.

If no other business offers itself, he sallies forth to look for cruelists. Very little has reached the public concerning Henry Bergh's personality. Photographers and portrait painters find him implacable. When several influential gentlemen proposed to erect a bronze statue to his honor, he said: "No, gentlemen, your well-meant kindness would injure the cause." Henry Bergh believes that fate called him to his work, and that nature expressly fitted him for it. It gave him an imposing stature and muscular strength. Circumstances provided him with the power of honest money and the travels and ambitions of his early life educated him in experience of men and the world, and for successful effort on the platform and at the bar.

If men are what they are born, a theory growing in popularity, Henry Bergh's obligations to his ancestors can be plainly traced. He was born in the city of New York, of rich but honest parents, in 1823, but since he was once heard to remark, "Age is a point I'm very tender upon. I'm never going to be more than forty-five," each reader is left to solve the easily formed equation.

One hundred and fifty years ago his German ancestors emigrated from the banks of the Rhine and settled on the Hudson. His father, Christian Bergh, who died about twenty-five years ago at the age of eighty-three, was regularly apprenticed when a boy to a builder of small vessels. After attaining by degrees the position of master carpenter, he began business for himself, eventually establishing a ship-yard at the foot of Scammel Street, East River, opposite the Navy Yard. When he died he was called the senior member of his craft, and had built more ships than any other ship-master in the country.

For several years he was in the service of the Government; he built the frigate President during the war of 1812, when the American navy astonished the world by its valor. Ill-luck, however, quickly overtook the President. The treaty of Ghent was signed in December14. During the following month, both sides being ignorant of the treaty of peace, the President, in attempting to put to sea from New York Harbor, was pursued by the English frigate Endymion of forty guns. The President showed fight and might have come off victorious but for the arrival of other vessels that hastened to aid the Endymion, compelling

Commodore Decatur to strike his colors. Years ago, when Henry Bergh was riding on the Thames in a yacht, he steamed under the oaken bows of the President, then a hoary captive still pulling at the anchors that chained her to foreign waters.

Christian Bergh built several of the Greek frigates that fought in the war of deliverance with Turkey. He was a man of iron will and steadfastness of purpose. As tall as his son, his dignified stature and long white hair gave him the appearance of a patriarch. He was a member of Tammany Hall, and because he could not be induced to take office, was a favorite with the society, and was usually asked to preside at public meetings. The idol of his soul was honesty, and his acute dread of being in debt, for a man in his circumstances, was a curious virtue. On his deathbed, it troubled him to think that he might die before his physicians were paid, and his son was compelled to draw a check to their order to calm the steadfast spirit in its last moments on earth. It was the verdict of the press that a useful man and a great builder of ships had passed away, and that he was known to be a perfectly honest man.

Henry Bergh once said that the most of what was in him that was good he owed to his mother, who was Elizabeth Ivers, the daughter of a Connecticut family, an amiable and excellent woman and a devoted Christian. The fortune of the great ship-builder was shared by three children, of whom the daughter died in middle life. Henry Bergh entered Columbia College, but before he had completed his course or his minority made his first visit to Europe. Shortly after his return, in his twenty-fifth year, he married a New York lady, the daughter of Thomas Taylor, her parents being English. During a residence of twelve years abroad, during which period he returned home at intervals, he visited every part of the Continent, and traveled extensively in the East.

Literature was the object of Henry Bergh's youthful ambition, and he pursued it till well advanced in life. He had a strong desire to succeed as a playwright, and wrote poetry. Ten or twelve plays are the fruit of his foreign leisure, and they abound in genuine humor. London dramatists have commended them, but managers here were loath to attempt their representation. One of his shortest pieces was acted with some success in Philadelphia. Among his unpublished plays are *Human Chattels*, written for a New York manager and satirizing the mania of American mothers for securing alliances of their daughters with the pauper nobility of Europe; *A Decided Scamp*, a comedietta; *An Extraordinary Envoy*, a melodrama, and *Peculiar People*, a comedy. He has published a book of tales and sketches, including *The Streets of New York*, *The Ocean Paragon*, *The Portentous Telegram*, and a Serb-comic drama in five acts, blank verse, entitled *Loves Alternative*, the scene of which is the terrace and castle of Lahneck on the Rhine, opposite Stolzenfels, a ruin which Mr. Bergh once could have purchased for $100; in the play it is supposed to have been purchased and rebuilt by an English earl. Nearly twenty years ago he published in London a poem called *Married Off* dealing with the same subject of marriage with noble tramps. Mr. Bergh still adheres to the opinion that it was not a bad poem, but the London critics handled it without mercy. He went at once in anguish of spirit to his publisher in Cheapside, with numerous newspaper slips in his hand.

"Look at that!" he cried to the cheerful bookman. "They have literally skinned me alive." Taking him apart, Cheapside wisdom remarked, consolingly: "I will give you a little advice that may serve you well through life. If you are bound to appear in print, well and good if the newspapers speak in praise of you; but, next to praise, being cut to pieces is the best thing to be hoped for. What we have to fear most is that we won't be noticed at all."

His experienced pen has been of vast service to him in his philanthropic work. Whisperings of his true mission in life came to Henry Bergh about the time of his appointment as Secretary of Legation at St. Petersburg in 1862. For years he had taken note of the cruelties practiced on dumb animals in European countries, and the brutal sports in which animal life was sacrificed. His strong sense of justice and human obligation led him to regard such cruelty as one of the greatest blemishes on human character.

In Russia the common people have, or had, a profound respect for official position. Mr. Bergh's footman wore the gold lace that served to distinguish members of the diplomatic corps. One day he interfered in behalf of a donkey that was being cruelly beaten, and made the happy discovery that the owner of the beast, as well as the crowd, stood in awe of the gold lace of his equipage. "At last," he said, "I've found a way to utilize my gold lace, and about the best use that can be made of it." So he formed a society of two, his coachman as executive officer, sympathizing in the work for the protection of dumb animals.

During his daily drives, if Mr. Bergh saw an animal in the toils of a cruelist, he would order his coachman to take the human brute into a side street and give him a regular blowing up. This and the gold lace always had the desired effect, though, so far as Mr. Bergh could understand, his coachman might have been reciting pastoral poetry in an off-hand way.

Mr. Bergh and his wife found the out-door climate of St. Petersburg beneficial, but the in-door climate was very damaging to health, owing to the double windows and to the large furnaces that burned all the oxygen out of the atmosphere. He was forced to resign his office on account of ill health, though he was much pleased with the country, as the Russian officials were with him, for he received the extraordinary compliment of having the emperor's yacht placed at his disposal to visit the naval station of Cronstadt. The vessel on this occasion carried the American flag.

Secretary Seward in accepting Mr. Bergh's resignation wrote that the government did so with great reluctance. Before leaving Russia he determined to devote the remainder of his life to the interests of dumb animals, and on his way home stopped in London to confer with Lord Harrowby, president of the English [animal protection] society that was afterward Mr. Bergh's model. He landed at New York in the autumn of 1864 and spent a year in maturing his plans. First of all, he took himself aside, as it were, and scrupulously inquired if he had the strength to carry on such a work and the ability to make the necessary sacrifices. He concluded that he was equal to the task.

A paper now hangs on the walls of the office bearing the signatures of seventy citizens of New York and inspiring almost as much reverence of a kind as the Declaration of Independence. It proclaims the duty of protecting animals from cruelty, and among the signers are Horace Greeley, Peter Cooper, George Bancroft, John A. Dix, Henry W. Bellows, Mayor Hoffman, John Jacob Astor and Alexander T. Stewart. After procuring this paper; Mr. Bergh next prepared a charter and Laws, and successfully urged their passage at Albany. On the evening of February 8th, 1866, Mayor Hoffman, A.T. Stewart and a few other gentlemen, came through rain and six inches of slush to listen to Mr. Bergh at Clinton Hall. In the following April the society was legally organized, Henry Bergh being elected president and George Bancroft a vice-president. At the close of his brief address the enthusiastic president cried: "This, gentlemen, is the verdict you have this day rendered, that the blood-red hand of cruelty shall no longer torture dumb beasts with impunity."

That same evening Henry Bergh buttoned his overcoat and went forth to defend the laws he had been mainly instrumental in securing, aware that on himself more than on any other man depended whether they were laughed at or obeyed. They were a radical innovation, for up to 1865 no law for the protection of animals from cruelty could be found on the statute book of any state in the Union. The common law regarded animals simply as property, and their masters, in wanton cruelty, or anger (for which Rozan, the French moralist, says there is no better definition than temporary insanity), might torture his sentient chattels without legal hindrance or accountability.

Henry Bergh put on this new armor of the law to battle no less for humanity than for dumb animals. A timely arrival at Fifth Avenue and Twenty-Second Street, where a brutal driver was beating a lame horse with the butt-end of a whip resulted in an indecisive skirmish. He tried to reason with the man, who simply laughed in derision and offered to pommel him if he would step into the street. Mr. Bergh went home reflecting that there was a material difference between brute protection in America, where every man felt that he was something of a king, and in Russia, where there were gold lace and a submissive peasantry.

The next day, from an omnibus, he saw a butcher's wagon loaded with live sheep and calves, thrown together like so much wood, their heads hanging over the edges of the wagon box and their large innocent eyes pleading in dumb agony. He alighted, and made a sensation by arresting the butcher and taking him before a magistrate, but New York justice was not at that time quite prepared to act without a precedent.

Early in May Mr. Bergh succeeded in having a Brooklyn butcher fined for similar acts of cruelty, and numerous arrests, resulting in a few convictions, were made in New York. He visited the marketplaces and the river piers and walked the busy streets, searching his brains for some means of bringing his cause prominently before the people.

One morning, late in May, he saw a schooner just arrived in port from Florida with a cargo of live turtles that had made the passage on their backs, their flippers having been pierced and tied with strings. Seeing his opportunity to make a stir, Mr. Bergh arrested the captain and the entire crew for cruelty to animals and marched them into court, the judge sharing the amusement of the spectators and the lawyers. The captains counsel urged that turtles were not animals within the meaning of the law, but fish, and if they were animals the treatment was not cruelty because painless. The learned judge, in giving a decision favorable to the prisoners, said it was past his belief that cruelty could have been inflicted on the turtles when the sense of pain caused by boring holes in their fins was about what a human being would experience from a mosquito bite.

Professor Agassiz afterward came to Henry Bergh's assistance in the long struggle to make it legally apparent, as the latter said, if not otherwise, to the torturers of the poor despised turtle, that the great Creator, in endowing it with life, gave to it feeling and certain rights, as well as to ourselves. Mr. Bennett had already begun in his newspaper to ridicule the society and Mr. Bergh as the Moses of the movement, while a little later he aided the cause with money. He did the greatest possible good to the movement, however, two or three days after the turtle suit, by publishing a satire several columns long, purporting to be a report of a mass meeting of animals at Union Square, Mr. Bergh in the chair. Each animal expressed his honest conviction concerning the work, and the article was so amusing and keen that before forty-eight hours had passed Mr. Bergh and his society had engaged the attention of perhaps half a million people.

From that day the cause moved steadily forward. By August the new society was in a flourishing condition financially, Mr. and Mrs. Bergh having bequeathed a valuable property to it. Drinking fountains for horses and dogs were placed on the streets in convenient and thronged localities. That ubiquitous and humane biped, as Mr. Bergh was called, was attacked for inconsistency in not interfering against the wholesale slaughter of dogs in the city pound. He replied: "It does not necessarily follow that there is cruelty in taking animal life; otherwise the butcher exposes himself to this charge, and all who eat flesh are to a certain extent, accomplices. In the case of the dogs, it is more a question of death than cruelty, and I am free to confess that I am not quite satisfied in my own mind whether life or speedy dissolution is most to be coveted by man or beast in this hot and disagreeable world."

This was a summer of many discouragements, and his words were, as to the last sentiment, doubtless colored by his disappointment. His wife, who has been a tower of encouragement and never-failing source of sympathy, once said, when there was no further need of concealing a noble weakness, that her husband had many a night come home so burdened with injury and disappointment that he would go upstairs to his room and have a jolly good cry. Yet the next morning always found him going forth with new courage to face the rebuffs of another day. In November, 1866, was begun a controversy with the professors of the medical colleges on the subject of vivisection. It was kept up at intervals, for several years, Mr. Bergh maintaining his position against vivisection, except with the use of anesthetics, in several eloquent letters, saying, in one of the first, "I protest in the name of heaven, public morality, and of this society against these fearful cruelties inflicted on dumb, unresisting creatures confided to the merciful protection of mankind."

In Mr. Bergh's office may be seen a lithograph portrait of Majendie, who appears to be as handsome and as finely organized a person as Washington Irving. Underneath the picture, in Mr. Bergh's bold

Thomas Nast pictures "Mr. Bergh to the Rescue"
The Defrauded Gorilla: That *Man* wants to claim my Pedigree.
  He says he is one of my Descendants.
Mr. Bergh: Now, Mr. Darwin, how could you insult him so?

Cartoonist pokes fun at Bergh's beliefs and mission.

handwriting, is this scathing commentary: A French physiologist, otherwise known as the Prince of Brute Torturers, who dissected, alive, 40,000 dumb animals, and ere he died confessed that vivisection was a failure!! During the three years following, Mr. Bergh had use for all his pluck and courage. In the final of dealers who had been detected in mixing marble dust with horse feed, Mr. Bergh, as usual, conducted the prosecution himself, and being called to task in court for his personal interference, exclaimed: "I stand here as a humble defender of the much-injured brute creation. I am here as an advocate for the people." To the Superintendent of Police he wrote, on deep provocation: "I claim a right not only to the assistance of your officers, but also especially to exemption from contempt and insult." At another time he says: "Two or three years of ridicule and abuse have thickened the epidermis of my sensibilities, and I have acquired the habit of doing the thing I think right, regardless of public clamor."

By persistent interference on behalf of lame and overloaded car-horses he made himself the object of much abuse and opposition, but finally corrected the shameful evil and gained at least the outward respect of horse-railway companies. The president of an east-side railroad made a futile effort to have him convicted for obstructing travel. In 1872, when the horse epidemic was so prevalent and fatal, Mr. Bergh worked with tireless energy. As at other strategic points, he stood at the Bowery and Fifth street, where two lines converge, stopping every down car with a sick horse attached, and compelling the passengers to alight. "If we are a civilized and Christian people," he would say to, them, "let us show it now and walk." Public opinion sustained him. Such incidents as follow, were of frequent occurrence in his daily life. One June morning he met, opposite the City Hall, two men leading a cow and her young calf. The cow's udder was frightfully distended, the calf having been kept from her to make the purchaser think she was a great giver of milk. Mr. Bergh ordered the men to let the calf have suck under penalty of arrest.

"The animals are mine," said the owner, reluctantly obeying.

"Yes," replied the philanthropist; "that may be, but the milk is Nature's and belongs to the famishing little creature that is now drinking it." He kept the men, in the presence of a large crowd till the calf, butting and tugging, and frisking its tail in vealy ecstasy, had satisfied its hunger. He has often compelled the milking of cows in the streets when the udders were unnaturally distended. One day, a poor emaciated horse fell at Duane Street, on Broadway. Before the officer, who went for means to shoot the horse, had returned, Mr. Bergh had procured hay, oats and water for the starving animal, which, after a few hours rest and feed, was able to get up and walk home.

During the erection of a brick building in Walker street, an inquisitive cat crawled into the large hollow iron girder, supporting the front of the building above the first story, and the workmen, either by wicked intent or by accident, walled up the open end, consigning the cat to a lingering death. The masons gave no heed to the animal's cries, and laid tier after tier of the front walls. Two or three days afterward a gentleman who was passing, hearing the piteous cries, learned the cause, and sent for Mr. Bergh. The latter called upon the owners of the building, who were unwilling to bear the expense of taking down the walls.

"How can you hope," said Mr. Bergh, "to prosper in your business with such a crime sealed up in your building? How can you ever enter it without thinking of the cries of this perishing creature? If the walls were built to the cornice, I would still compel you to render justice to humanity. Order those walls taken down at once, or I will have you punished by the law." They obeyed, and the cat, after a long last, was taken out, with three of its nine lives apparently intact.

As soon as Mr. Bergh saw his way clear to success he began a vigorous crusade against the dog-fighters, rat-baiters and cock-fighters, who carried on their brutal sports in the vilest quarters of the city with little attempt at secrecy. Within two or three years these degrading exhibitions were almost banished from Manhattan Island, and Mr. Bergh carried the war into Brooklyn and Westchester County. With dauntless bravery, himself and agents, sometimes making a party of three or five, would make a descent on a dog-pit where one or two hundred of the roughest men were gathered, and break up the fight, always making numerous arrests. Their success was complete in New York, but dog and cock fighting still prevail on the outskirts of Brooklyn, in which city Mr. Bergh has been compelled, from lack of the support of the authorities, almost to abandon all effort.

One of the greatest services rendered to New York was the exposure and prosecution of those who were engaged in the swill milk crime. Cows were kept in stables under ground and fed upon garbage and distillery slops. Sometimes the animals were so diseased that they had to be supported by belts from the ceiling. The New York public was horrified by the revelations made. But in his report for 1877, Mr. Bergh says: "Swill milk still continues to be one of the preferred beverages of Long Island, and in deference to the popular aphorism, vox populi suprema lex, we have determined not to interfere further with their enjoyment of it."

He wrote a letter to the farmers of Long Island asking them to co-operate against the attempt to introduce foxhunting as a sport, but could awaken no

Only two horses for the load

Overloaded horse cart in New York. (Courtesy of ASPCA Archives.)

enthusiasm. He calls Long Island the jumping-off place, and has predicted that it will be taken possession of some day by all the thieves and desperate tramps of the country who will entrench themselves and defy the whole power of government. "Figs do not grow on thistles," he says, "and if the devil be at the head of a people it is simply because the people are devilish."

In suppressing pigeon shooting he had to confront the influence of wealth and position, and to encounter many personal indignities, but he succeeded as in everything else that he has undertaken. Hollow glass balls thrown from spring traps now frequently take the place of the live birds. By impartial arrest he compelled wealthy residents to blanket clipped horses in cold weather. The coachmen of the city, mostly without the knowledge of their employers, began using a round leather bit-guard, barbed with short spikes, so that when the reins were tightened, the nails sunk into the side of the horses head, and made the animal exhibit a very fashionable degree of mettle. These were discovered and quickly captured. So considerate is this class now, that if a peculiar check-rein or binding-strap is used on a coach-horse to correct pulling on the bit or other equine foibles, the horse is often driven to the society's offices to get Mr. Bergh's sanction.

At the outset, Henry Bergh found it necessary to attend personally to the prosecution of cruelty cases in the courts, for humane feeling and moral courage were more useful than profound legal knowledge to secure legal penalties, without which his society and his laws, no less than himself, would soon have become failures. To enable him to practice as counsel for the prosecution of cruelty cases in the courts, the Attorney General of the state and the District Attorney of the county clothed him with representative power. His clear, impressive voice is still heard almost from day to day in the Court of Sessions, where he has done some of his most valuable and characteristic work.

Mr. Bergh was once brought up for contempt of court because he wrote a letter to a grand jury, but the strong effort made to punish him for this failed. Once when a New Jersey magistrate refused to sentence a man who had been guilty of great cruelty, Mr. Bergh wrote him a very sharp letter, saying: "Next time, if you will not do your duty in the premises, I shall take measures to punish you legally." New Jersey justice was not always indifferent. A young man in Hackensack was courting a young lady in Paterson, and because the drive was a long one and a cold one, would bask unconscionably long in the beams of his sweethearts countenance, leaving his horse to starve and shiver in the wind. The magistrate, before whom the lover was taken, cooled his ardor with a fine of twenty-five dollars and costs.

From time to time unscrupulous newspapers attacked Mr. Bergh on various grounds. Most frequently he was accused of inflicting cruelty on human beings in his over zeal to protect animals. But, in fact, he has been very considerate, and has privately shown charity. One day he saw from his window a skeleton horse, scarcely able to drag a rickety wagon and the poverty stricken driver. Mr. Bergh hastened out, and said: "You ought not to compel this horse to work in his present condition."

"I know that," answered the man, "but look at the horse, look at the wagon, look at the harness, and then look at me, and say, if you can, which of us is most wretched." Then he drew up the shirt-sleeve of one arm, and continued: "Look at this shrunken limb past use; but I have a wife and two children at home, as wretched as we here, and just as hungry."

"Come with me," Mr. Bergh replied, "I have a stable down this street; come and let me give one good square meal to your poor horse, and something to yourself and family." He placed oats and hay before the stay of the family, and a generous sum of money in the hand of the man. He has often pleaded in court for some person arrested for cruelty, whose miserable poverty and the dependence of wife and children were made to appear by the testimony.

In Mr. Bergh's office hangs the portrait of a man of almost repulsive features, in whose countenance there is yet something peculiarly attractive and re-assuring. It is Louis Bonard, next to Mr. Bergh the society's chief benefactor. He was a Frenchman who, leaving Rouen a poor man, came to this country, and made a fortune in trafficking with, the Indians, which he greatly increased by judicious investments in New York real estate. When he was taken sick in 1871 and removed to St. Vincent's Hospital he sent for Mr. Bergh, who happened to be in Washington but soon returned. Bonard, at his own request had a will drawn bequeathing his entire property, $150,000, to the society, believing, as he said, that he had no relatives living. After his death Mr. Bergh saw him decently buried in Greenwood, near Battle Avenue, and erected a monument to his memory. In his memorandum book, over a space of a few years, was found occasional mention of Mr. Bergh's name but no commentary.

Alleged relatives in Rouen endeavored to break the will on the assumption that Bonard was a believer in metempsychosis or the doctrine of transmigration of souls. A long litigation confirmed the Society's right to the property.

Similar interest in animals is not infrequent. It was a New Jersey bachelor who left $400,000 for the use, benefit and behoove of his horses for ten years, his relations being put off for that length of time.

A French lady offered to leave $20,000 to the society. Wills aggregating half a million dollars in bequests have been drawn by philanthropic men still living, in favor of the Society, which now needs ready money more than the prospect of stepping into dead men's shoes. Before the Bonard bequest the Society lived in a little upstairs room at Broadway and Fourth Street, plainly furnished with a manila carpet and a few chairs. No room of its size on this continent, it was admitted, wielded the same power and moral influence.

Mr. Bergh could look out of his window and note the condition of passing horses. During heavy snowstorms, he would stand in the street protected by a heavy coat and top boots. Once, when the snow was ten inches deep, he turned back every stage, compelled the passengers to walk, and in this work finally reached Union Square, where the crowd of people that had gathered gave him three rousing cheers. With the Bonard money available it was decided to seek more imposing quarters. The building at Fourth Avenue and Twenty-second Street was purchased and decorated according to Mr. Bergh's plan, so as to attract the attention of all passers-by and remind them of the Society and its work.

In 1874, Mr. Bergh rescued two little girls from inhuman women, most notably the shockingly treated little Mary Ellen. This led to the founding of a Society for the Prevention of Cruelty to Children. The previous year he made a lecturing tour over the principal cities of the West, which resulted in the formation of several societies for the prevention of cruelty to animals. He spoke twice before committees of the Evangelical Alliance and once before the Episcopal Convention, which confirmed a new canon to the effect that Protestant Episcopal ministers should, at least once a year, preach a sermon on cruelty and mercy to animals. He has often addressed school children, and frequently advocated the cause of the animals in pulpit and on platform.

Elbridge T. Gerry, the legal counselor of the Society and a grandson of the signer of the Declaration of Independence, whose name he bears, is a self-sacrificing co-worker. A neat illustrated journal, called Our Animal Friends, is published under the auspices of the Society, and is now in its sixth year. Henry Bergh and his officers cannot be everywhere at once, but they sometimes think that some mysterious providence leads them to cases of cruelty, so successful are they in being at the right place at the right time.

All members of the Society have a badge of authority, and frequently supplement the officers' efforts. Many gentlemen with no authority assume it. In January last a Broad street merchant was seen to rush out of his office into the street and shake his fist at a teamster sitting on fifteen bales of cotton, with his truck fast in the snow, the merchant exclaiming: "You ruffian! Stop licking those horses, or Ill have you locked up!" The driver stopped. Two ambulances for disabled horses are now kept ready for public use. When the ambulance was first introduced, it was passing Wallack's Theatre one evening with a noble white horse that had been injured, standing in it. The novel spectacle attracted the crowds that were passing into the theater. They turned around, waited for the cavalcade to pass, and gave three cheers for the Society. A clergyman once said: "That ambulance preaches a better sermon than I can."

Devices for raising animals out of street excavations and various other appliances are kept at the principal office. Every few days the superintendent, with an officer, drives at six o'clock in the morning to the pork-packing establishments on the west side, where horses are made to draw enormous loads; then to the trains at Forty-first Street, where live hogs are unloaded; thence down the west side, stopping at all the Jersey ferries to examine the milk-cart horses, and truck horses; thence to Washington Market and Fulton Market to look at the peddlers' horses, getting back to the office at nine o'clock, ready for the daily routine.

Up to the present time, the society has interfered, without making arrests, to prevent seventeen thousand disabled animals from being worked, and has prosecuted in over six thousand cases of cruelty. Great as are the material benefits society derives from Henry Bergh's work, in the economy of animal life, the moral benefits obtained are vastly greater. Indeed, the work was first rendered possible by the liberation of the slave, because a reasonable people could not have listened to the claims of dumb animals while human beings, held in more ignoble bondage, were subjected to greater cruelty and added outrage. He took up the principles of humanity, for which two chief martyrs fell, crowned with human love, and is carrying them forward by teaching men to be noble and strong through pity and self restraint.

4

Mr. Bergh, Won't You Help The Children?

While Bergh was intent on limiting the scope of his efforts to the saving of animals, a large contingency of the public would not accept that. The newspaper articles that follow chronicle much of the pressure Bergh experienced after founding the ASPCA in April of 1866.

Home Journal, June 20, 1866. H.A. Delille

A WORD FOR THE CHILDREN

While so much has been accomplished, there yet remains room for a vast improvement upon this prevention-of-cruelty movement. We refer to the cases of infantile distress and misery, of abject destitution, of fearful cruelty endured by hundreds of little beings who are the more to be noticed and cared for that they have souls within those poor little bodies. Alas! Who has not seen these miserable children (animals we might call them) in their degraded, suffering ignorance and vice. They are the tortured of older vagrants – ruffianly beings of both sexes, who, when young, were alike cruelly treated, and who now repay in kind, the violence, the wrongs committed against them in past days. The little wretches we are referring to are met with in all our streets; they are dirty, half-starved, precocious, cunning and vicious. They beg with a pertinacity that will scarcely accept a refusal. In winter, thinly clad and barefooted, they shock even the most thoughtless into painful reflections as to the state of society that permits these exhibitions of poverty and want. To satisfy that prompting of conscience which teaches that such misery should not exist here, of all places in the world, we give away our pennies, knowing however, that the shivering little recipients thereof will not benefit thereby. No, these little beggars are but collecting "gin money" for the beasts in human form who drive them forth to seek so many pennies each day, or mercilessly beat and starve them. In many instances, the more unsophisticated, the kinder-hearted take these beggars and clothe them. The next day the little wretches are again in rags, and the pawnbrokers have obtained possession of the "nice warm things" the donors intended for the relief of the little ones. It often happens that these little beggars are pretty children, and that you feel unusually attracted by the sweet face and the wistful eyes. You question them and learn, as they feel instinctively that they may trust you, details which cause your blood to run cold, cruel welts across the little backs are shown to you, and recitals of frightful suffering render you furious. You complain to the police, but meet with chilling indifference, or with doubts, which exasperate you. You mention the mater to parties whom you know to be generous and influential, and obtain ready relief for the individual case of suffering which so grieved and interested you. For the time being, your satisfaction is great; but this subsides when, day after day, similar cases meet your observation, and you become aware that hundreds, nay thousands of little beings, are quite as miserable as the child you were instrumental in releasing. Before the magnitude of the evil you recoil, dismayed, and after many struggles, assume an indifference you scarcely feel. With pleasure you read in the morning papers that, by order of the Chief of Police, little vagrants and beggars will be arrested. This will put a stop to the vicious abuse of the children, and you are satisfied. A few days, or at least weeks, pass by; again you meet the little beggars. The wretches are not there voluntarily; their brutal parents or keepers have driven them out to beg or be beaten. T is for the relief of these "animals" that all would desire to see founded a "Society for the Prevention of Cruelty", having among its members wealthy and influential people who would fearlessly, and with determination, seek to protect the little ones. Each season collections of one dollar or less even, might be made from at least one hundred thousand persons in the city, and the money be applied to the relief, the clothing and housing of the cruelly persecuted children. We should thus be enabled to save many from after lives of sin; could bring refining influences to bear upon the susceptible minds which now know but sin and menace, and would insure the ultimate usefulness of those who, left to their present sufferings and teachings, can but grow up vile and corrupted. There are, it is true, houses of refuge and asylums; but these are places of charity; let there be a lawful interference in this matter; in short, let us have a legally constituted and organized "Society for the Prevention of Cruelty to Children."

This next article was clipped from the newspaper by Bergh, and inserted in his scrapbook. Notes he jotted on the article will appear in italics and in [*brackets*]. The article is from 1867, and shows that while child abuse was common, there was no legal method to protect them from their parents and guardians:

New York Sun, *February 12, 1867*

MORE CHILD BEATING

The Columbus Ohio Journal of last week relates the following: Mrs. Fanny Blackburn, a resident of Middletown, was arrested on Saturday for inhumanly whipping and beating her child, a little girl of 6 or 7 years of age. This punishment was not the result of a single fit of rage, but the child had been mistreated by both father and mother for two or three weeks. The neighbors had frequently protested, but had only met with insult from the parents. On Saturday morning, the cries of the child brought the police to its rescue. The woman was arrested and taken to the city prison, and the child given into the care of some of the ladies living near. The woman at the mayor's office made no defense, but said that she punished the child to "make it mind". She was careful, when asked her name, to emphasize "Mrs. Fanny Blackburn." She spoke no word in explanation or in palliation of her crime. When the officer reported that the child would die in a few minutes, she showed no signs of emotion. Her face seemed that of a person much abused, and with no proper appreciation of the crime attached to the inhuman abuse of her child. She walked into the cell at the city prison in a calm matter-of-fact way, and scarcely heeded the expression of the officer that he must hurry away for a physician. Dr. Helmick first visited the child, and afterwards Dr. Boyle. The legs, arms and body of the child were bruised, as though beaten by a heavy stick or club, and upon the body there were one or two severe cuts, and a very severe cut upon the head, amounting almost to a fracture of the skull. The hands had been held to the hot stove until severely burned. On both sides of each hand there were bad looking blisters, and the mother admitted that she had resorted to this burning of the child's hands as a mode of punishment, but that she "didn't know the stove was so hot." [*This article is inserted to show a perfectly parallel case where an "Animal" has been abused by man; The animal flees from man; and only by kindness is made docile and useful.*] When the marshal and other officers entered the room, the little girl sprang from them, but when she was assured of their kindness, she was almost delirious in her manner of expressing her thankfulness. She seemed absolutely insane upon the subject of being whipped. Later in the day, her father, Thomas J. Blackburn, who was not allowed to go near his child, at the foundry where he was employed, made use of some unwarranted and insulting expressions in regard to the ladies in whose charge the girl had been placed, and two or three young fellows, some of the ladies referred to, proceeded to "trounce" him after the most approved style. The police interfered, and it was learned that he had abused the child as much as his wife, and as the feeling against them both was very bitter, he was arrested and taken to the calaboose. The child, in the afternoon, was taken to St. Frances' Hospital, at the Medical College, and hopes were yesterday entertained that it would recover, but with a deformed body and a weakened mind. The feeling against Blackburn and his wife in Middletown was of such a character that a prompt arrest saved them perhaps from a worse fate. The facts in the case afford their own comment.

Bergh continued to be a target of his critics. This article appeared in 1867, little more than a year after formation of the ASPCA:

Daily News, May 1867

Among the many useless and nonsensical laws now in force in this city and Brooklyn, none gives the people more trouble and does less good than that for the protection of dumb animals. A number of persons are arrested daily on frivolous charges of this nature, but they are generally discharged by the magistrates for want of proof of guilt. The people who are so tender about a broken-winded horse would find a wider field for their sympathy if they would pay a little more attention to the care of human beings.

And yet another plea for Bergh to help those *outside* the animal kingdom:

The New York Ledger, August 3, 1867 (Robert Bonner, Editor)

CRUELTY TO ANIMALS: ALSO TO WIVES AND CHILDREN
It is right that maltreated dumb creatures should have their wrongs avenged, and the society organized

THE ONLY MOURNER.

The cartoonist "Puck" shows Bergh chasing a dog catcher's cart.
(Courtesy of ASPCA Archives.)

for the purpose of protecting them and bringing their tormentors to grief deserves the countenance and encouragement of the public. The man who wantonly misuses a horse, or a dog, or any other animal, is prima facie a brute, and should be punished for his brutality. But when it comes to depriving the anaconda of his dinner of live spring chicken or rabbit, we hardly know what to say. Protest has been made in London against serving caged reptiles of the constrictor species with animated rations, and the protest has been repeated here; but it should be considered that if not allowed to butcher for themselves, they decline as persistently as if they were strait-laced Hebrews, to eat meat at all. Moreover, it is quite certain that in their native jungle they would have foraged on live stock. What then can be done? Would it be right, on the plea of humanity, to reduce the menagerie anaconda to the suicidal necessity of swallowing his own blanket in order to save from his clutches the fowl or rabbit which is sure to be killed under any circumstances? It is a nice case – susceptible to a world of moral illustration – and we leave its decision to the eminent philanthropists who have taken it in hand, feeling assured that equal and exact justice will be done to both sides, and not caring particularly which whips. Perhaps it would not be amiss to suggest in this connexion, that the Society for the Prevention of Cruelty to Animals should extend the sphere of its labors so as to include a few classes of ill-used bipeds – such as children who are unmercifully whipped and starved by their brutal parents; poor sewing girls who are swindled out of their hard earnings by soulless employers; broken-spirited wives who are habitually cuffed and kicked by drunken husbands, and the like. Nobody interferes to prevent such cruelties as these; and except in a few flagrant cases that force themselves upon the attention of the authorities, they are perpetrated with entire impunity. We submit that a cudgeled woman, or a flayed and starving child, or a seamstress swindled out of her daily bread, deserves commiseration as much as a horse with a sore back, or a leveret in a boa's cage.

The following editorial is with a different slant. The author is clearly concerned about the children of the well-to-do in the city, forced to wear fashionable, but weather-inappropriate clothes to please their mothers:

The Northern Budget, Troy, NY. December 22, 1867

CRUELTY TO CHILDREN

We believe that the Society for the Prevention of Cruelty to Animals has an agent in Troy who creditably represents President Bergh and his philanthropic associates. The health and treatment of the lower animals are being zealously looked after by the society. If a horse is beaten, or a cow confined in a narrow, unventilated stable, on learning the facts, the society straightaway makes complaint before a Magistrate and the brutal or negligent owner of the suffering animal is arrested, reprimanded, and fined. If a drove of sheep is hurried too rapidly through the streets, or an unoffending calf is tied foot to foot and thrown upon his back into a butcher's wagon, the society is on the alert, and the cruelty is punished. This is all right, so far as it goes, for although such laws may be made ridiculous for those charged with their execution, they are yet productive of much good in the aggregate. But the society does not extend the fields of its labors so far as it should. It is not alone the lower animals that are subject to ill treatment and cruelty, but man – the highest type of the animal creation – is also exposed to it.

A society for the prevention of cruelty to children would find a large field for labor. It is not enough to guard the interests of our horses, calves and lambs – the human lambs also require their care. It is doubtless very trying to these good-hearted old gentlemen to see a dray horse overladen, or witness the improper, injudicious tabling of a cow, but do they never in perambulating the busy streets, pause to look down upon the suffering, freezing children of aristocratic parents? If they do, they witness cruelty a thousand fold more reprehensible than that of which they daily complain. They will see in the coldest weather little children, with arms and legs bare – or almost bare – fashionably but scantily clothes, shivering in the rude blasts of winter, and taking into their systems the seeds of disease which in nineteen cases out of twenty hurry them to early graves, and in the twentieth, make them sufferers during life. And the guilty ones in these cases are not as might be supposed, the natural enemies of the little ones, but their mothers. Perhaps mothers do not know to what they are exposing their children, but they should be educated to know, or – failing in that – should be deprived of their care. If any of them doubt the pernicious affects of such child fashions, let them try the effect upon themselves some bitter winter day; let them go out upon the streets in dresses, reaching to the knee, thin stockings, light shoes, and bare arms, and then say if we are not right.

The pleas for Bergh and Gerry to intervene on behalf of the children seemed never ending. While it may seem Bergh was the focus of all the press attention, Gerry was hard at work behind the scenes. He was a private man, a dedicated legal advisor to Bergh, and one who did not desire the spotlight. He did not do much writing or public speaking, and interviews with the press are nearly non-existent. But he did help perpetrate the first attempt at the rescue of an abused child, discovering a particular section of the Writ of Habeas Corpus that might serve to help a child. Here is Emily Thompson's story:

*Child Abuse and Neglect*96, Stephen Lazoritz and Eric A. Shelman

BEFORE MARY ELLEN

When tracing the history of the child protection movement back to its origins, the case of 9-year-old Mary Ellen Wilson is almost unanimously acknowledged as the seminal case. The well-publicized case of "Little Mary Ellen" was monumental, being the impetus for the child protection movement in this country. It is not widely known, however, that Henry Bergh, founder of the American Society for the Prevention of Cruelty to Animals, had demonstrated his unique love for the rights of all creatures in another, earlier case of child abuse, the case of Emily Thompson. That first attempt to rescue a child from an abusive home was initially viewed as a failure, not only by his critics, but by Bergh himself. Since, however, it was the first case of child abuse in which Henry Bergh intervened, the Emily Thompson case is certainly of great historical importance. While all of the details of this case have not been identified, ample information has been found in the unpublished notes of Bergh biographer Edward P. Buffet, and from newspaper reports of that time.

Henry Bergh, having founded the American Society for the Prevention of Cruelty to animals in April 1866, made tremendous advancements in animal protection during the Society's inaugural year. Still, there were many who questioned his dedication to the protection of "dumb brutes", then one of the most commonly used terms referring to members of the animal kingdom. An example of this opinion is this letter, printed on May 1868 in the New York Telegram:

The New York Telegram, May 1868

WANTED: A CHILDREN'S CHAMPION – A
CHANCE FOR BERGH

Our model Christian, President Bergh, appears to have a hard time of it between blustering sea captains, burly butchers, refractory dog fanciers, and matter-of-fact police justices in his humane efforts to provide for the comfort of turtles, protect the interests of innocent calves, shield the ears of spaniels from the shears, and throw every person who is not as philanthropic and kind-hearted as himself into jail. It would not be surprising if he were to abandon his efforts on behalf of the brute creation in despair, and take to horse flesh as a diet for the remainder of his life.

But there is a field in which we believe Bergh might labor with more thanks for his pains and more success as his reward. The children of New York are sadly in want of a champion. They need a large heart and a resolute will to do battle in their behalf. The Central Park Commissioners hesitate about affording them all those amusements and privileges in the park to which we believe them entitled; the boarding house keepers and letters of lodgings in this city, with Nero-like barbarity, refuse to receive them under their roofs, and now the landlords of fashionable watering place hotels actually give notice of their intention to banish them from their establishments during the summer months. What are the little suffering martyrs to do? Must they remain staved up in unhealthy tenement houses in the close, hot city during all the beautiful of fruits and flowers? Is their interesting prattle no longer to be heard in the park, at the springs, or along the sea shore? Are they to be kept shut up like those birds in a cage, to pine away and die? Here is a splendid opportunity for Bergh. Children are more precious than turtles or turkeys, calves, cart horses, or black and tans; and if he will only open his large heart to the little ones, and insist that as all the happiness of life centers in them, so all its joys, pleasures and blessings should be showered upon their dear heads without stint and without grumbling, he will be entitled to and will receive the praise of all mankind – aye, and of all womankind as well.

The tone of the letter above seems to indicate that the author was not sympathetic to Bergh's cause. This article is representative of many other articles and editorials scornful of Bergh's society and its focus. Bergh once responded with this statement:

Human beings have enjoyed a monopoly [on kind treatment] from time immemorial, and now the day has arrived when the great mass of beings outside of mankind must be allowed some little share in the good things of life.

Perhaps the articles did have an affect on Henry Bergh, for in June of 1871, a woman entered Bergh's offices to ask that he intervene on behalf of eight year-old Emily Thompson. Bergh set aside his work for animals and listened to her appeal. The woman approached Bergh to intervene "Because, " she said, "a man who shows so much mercy to animals cannot be but equally kind to men." She told Bergh that from her window she could see into the yard next door. There, she frequently watched a woman brutally beat and whip a little girl, sometimes for up to an hour at a time. Though Bergh had previously stated that such cases ". . . were not in his particular line", he sent some of his agents to investigate, and found little Emily to be black and blue from the treatment. Several neighbors came forward to testify that they, too, had witnessed the beatings almost daily.

It is well documented that in 1874, Mary Ellen Wilson was removed from her abusive home by virtue of a writ of habeas corpus invoked by Elbridge T. Gerry, the S.P.C.A. 's young attorney. At the time of the Mary Ellen case, it was said to be an ingenious application of section 65 of the habeas corpus act, and Gerry was applauded for his work. However, no mention has ever been made as to the exact section of the writ used in the Emily Thompson case, so one can assume it was one and the same.

In any event, the writ was applied, and little Emily Thompson was removed from the abusive home and presented before Judge Barnard in the Court of Special Sessions. In court, the child's face and neck were severely bruised, showing clear evidence of malicious abuse. Mary Ann Larkin, the child's keeper, testified that Emily's parents, who had lived in Philadelphia, were both dead. During the trial, she further testified that Emily's grandmother, referred to only as Mrs. Bickom, was deceased. Larkin testified before the court that she had taken Emily into her home out of the kindness of her heart, an arrangement she made with the child's elderly grandmother before her death.

As happens commonly in abuse cases even today, Emily was understandably frightened, and vehemently denied ever being beaten by the woman. She also refused to be separated from the woman she thought of as her mother. Emily's denial of the abuses inflicted upon her notwithstanding, Judge Barnard found Larkin guilty as charged, using the testimony of the many neighbors who served as witnesses and the grievous condition of the girl as evidence. He suspended sentence and sent the girl back to live with Mrs. Larkin, presumably because she had no living relatives.

Bergh left the courthouse heavy-hearted. He had proved the abuse of the child, but to what end? Emily Thompson was to remain in the abusive home, and would likely suffer more maltreatment at the hands of Mary Ann Larkin.

The newspapers, while applauding his efforts on Emily's behalf, remained somewhat condescending where his usual focus was concerned, as is illustrated in this article in the Brooklyn Eagle on June 1871:

Mr. Bergh has taken a very important step. He has recognized the human race as animals. On Saturday he caused the arrest of a woman who, the kind-hearted complainants charge, had unmercifully beaten her child. If now Mr. Bergh proposes to enlarge the jurisdiction of his society so as to take notice of and prevent cruelty to human beings as well as to dumb beasts, his society and its work will be greatly magnified. The occasions for interference will be indefinitely multiplied, because ill treatment of men, women, and children is probably more frequent and more outrageous than abuse of horses, dogs, cats, roosters, etc. In the particular case referred to, nothing came of the arrest, because the child positively denied that she had been cruelly beaten, and refused to be protected by being separated from her mother. The complainants wasted their sympathy and had their trouble for nothing – unless they found sufficient reward in a fresh lesson of the inexpediency of interfering in family differences. Still, it is something to know Mr. Bergh regards people as animals.

Facing the sneers of much of the press, Henry Bergh must have had some difficulty accepting the outcome, and quite possibly might have used the Thompson case as further reason for limiting his attention to the defense of the speechless who could not deny their abuses in court.

But the power of the press eventually worked in Bergh's favor. An elderly woman came to his offices one afternoon, a newspaper article tucked into her purse. She pulled it out and showed it to Bergh, identifying herself as Mrs. Bickom, little Emily's grandmother. She told Bergh she lived in Cape May, New Jersey, and strongly objected to Mary Ann Larkin's testimony that she was deceased. The 80-year-old woman had read about the case in the newspaper and despite her old age, left for Bergh's offices in New York the next day.

Mrs. Bickom confirmed that she agreed to allow Mrs. Larkin to raise her grandchild on the solemn promise she would treat her as her own daughter. Shortly after the arrangement was made, however, Larkin told her the child had died. She told Emily a similar story, and from that day forward, the child had no one but her.

Bergh immediately took Mrs. Bickom to Judge Barnard, and upon hearing the story, Barnard again invoked a writ of habeas corpus, removing Emily from Larkin's home and placing her with her natural grandmother. They returned together to New Jersey. Mary Ann Larkin never served time in prison for her actions.

Though the case of Mary Ellen Wilson led to the founding of the New York Society for the Prevention of Cruelty to Children in 1874 and is acknowledged as being the beginning of the child protection movement in this country, the case of Emily Thompson was, to the best of our knowledge, the first case in this country in which a child was removed from their home and brought to a court of law because of physical abuse. The case of Emily Thompson set the stage for Mary Ellen Wilson's well-publicized rescue, and in itself should be looked upon as an historic event.

And finally, in January of 1872, this letter appeared in the newspaper:

New York Times, January 27, 1872

Mr. Bergh - Dear Sir:

Everyone with a human heart must acknowledge and bless you for the good work you have done in this city. But shall this work end here? I cannot think you will allow it to do so. Can you not prevent the cruelty used toward the little children in our streets? Sufferers as powerless to help themselves as the dumb brutes, and yet with a far greater capacity for suffering. Probably there is no greater wrong than arises from the drugging of babies and small children by the beggars in our streets. On Fourteenth street may be seen daily a woman with three children, all drugged and placed in most agonizing positions. Think of the suffering endured when these children come out of the stupor - think of the pain in mind and body. Of course, the brain becomes diseased from this long-continued drugging, and when the child has grown too large to be longer useful as an object of pity, it is sent adrift on the world, distorted in soul, mind, and body.

This woman is only one out of a hundred instances. There is a man on Broadway with two children by his side, and I have seen him strike the little ones for stirring. I complained of him to a policeman, but it was of no avail. Now, I speak to you to ask if you cannot have these wretches arrested and sent where they will have to work, and the poor children placed in an asylum of some kind.

In prosecuting your work of mercy for dumb creatures, do not forget the creature whom God made in his own image, and to whom He has given a soul that may be saved by saving his body. These dumb creatures will not meet you in the life to come, but if you rescue but one human being, angels will envy you your reward.

A LADY WHO IS DEEPLY INTERESTED

Two years later the NYSPCC would come into being, and the concerned woman who wrote the letter above would have her wish granted. Though Henry Bergh was responsible for founding the NYSPCC with Elbridge T. Gerry, he did not wish to be president of the organization and insisted on maintaining it as a separate entity from his ASPCA. Bergh was certain that if the animal and child protection societies were joined, the children's needs would take precedence over those of the animals. He was strongly opposed to organizations that included animals and children under the moniker "Humane Society", and voiced his concerns many times over. Here is one letter found in Edward Buffet's collection of documents, this one in Henry Bergh's handwriting:

E.T. Gerry Esq.
1 April80

President of the New York Society for the Prevention of Cruelty to Children

My dear Mr. Gerry,

I am not in a condition of body to warrant my attending the meeting today; and if I were just to myself, I should have quitted the pernicious influence of March winds long ago for the more genial climate of the south. I however desire to invite your notice, and always opposed that of the Board of Directors of your Society, [illegible] to a course of policy, on its part – inaugurated [illegible] if I mistake not by our energetic Secretary – tending to the extinguishment of the Society for the Prevention of Cruelty to Animals

Mary Ellen's suitcase and the dress that she wore into the courthouse upon her rescue remain in the possession of the NYSPCC in New York City. (Photo by Eric Shelman)

by substituting, the one for the Protection of Children. This seeming propagandism is entirely gratuitous and needless; for the reason that there is work enough for both our Institutions everywhere; and its tendency, as already manifested, threatens, as you can easily conceive, to exterminate, if persisted in, that Society with which the natural and inherent selfishness of mankind is least closely allied.

By referring to your last Report, you will discover the fatal consequence of that policy to which I allude; where it is shown that already seven Societies, originally founded through the influence and example of the one over which I preside; have been alienated from their allegiance to the cause which first called them into being.

I have always opposed the amalgamation of these two Societies – and I think my opposition has been shared by you. While at the convention held at Baltimore two years since, I felt it my duty to protest against the views of your Secretary, as expressed by him, on that occasion, and subsequent reflection and experience confirm me in the correctness of such opposition.

As a co-laborer in the work of mercy and protection of all sentient beings from cruelty – without regard to race – I respectfully ask that both our Societies be allowed to prosecute their beneficent missions without hindrance or impediment from either.

Very Sincerely Yours,
Henry Bergh

In all fairness, while Bergh and Gerry had their differences over the years, Gerry's dedication and generosity to the ASPCA was truly appreciated by Bergh. Here is a public thank you that appeared in the Seventh Annual Report of the ASPCA:

MR. ELBRIDGE T. GERRY

To his eminent professional abilities, zeal, perseverance, and devotion to this God-approving work of defending the defenseless, the Society and its cause owe a debt inappreciable in dollars. I think that if I had ever been skeptical of the eternal presence of an overruling Providence in the affairs of this world, my repeated experience in the progress of this work would alone suffice to extinguish all doubt. How often, during its inception and development, have the dark clouds which lowered over my path suddenly and most unexpectedly opened, and the aid and support so coveted, and which rendered me for the time so despondent, have cleared them away. I regard this excellent gentleman as a signal manifestation of that Devine Sovereignty to which I allude. Not only have his prudent and sagacious counsels prevented or parried harm, but by his eloquent and astute advocacy of the rights of the Society before the judicial tribunals of the State, he has in some instances affirmed its powers, and preserved to its treasury that material element of success which, it is my melancholy duty to record, has prompted so many able yet selfish contestants to endeavor to divert from its sacred and humane destination, to their own personal uses. His skill and industry, however, were not sufficient to avert a loss of some thirty thousand dollars to the bequest of Mr. Bonard, all consumed in claims, court charges, and allowances to counsel – with one single exception – for the appreciable service of having stopped the realization of the dead mans holy desire for the pace of more than two years!

Henry Bergh shared his ASPCA offices with the NYSPCC until enough funds were acquired through donations to move the fledgling organization to its own building. A wealthy Quaker, John D. Wright, became the NYSPCC's first president, to be followed by Elbridge T. Gerry, who would lead the organization for nearly two more decades, even as he continued to volunteer his legal services to the ASPCA. And though he felt it necessary to continue drawing the line between the two societies for the protection of both, Bergh remained a member of the NYSPCC board until his death in 1888.

5

Press Coverage, April 10

New York Times, April 10, 1874

> MR. BERGH ENLARGING HIS SPHERE OF
> USEFULNESS
> Inhuman Treatment of a Little Waif – Her
> Treatment – A Mystery To Be Cleared Up

It appears from proceedings had in Supreme Court . . .
yesterday, in the case of a child named Mary Ellen, that
Mr. Bergh does not confine the humane impulses of his
heart to smoothing the pathway of the brute creation
toward the grave or elsewhere, but that he embraces
within the sphere of his kindly efforts the human
species also.   On his petition a special warrant was
issued by Judge Lawrence, bringing before him
yesterday the little girl in question, the object of Mr.
Bergh being to have her taken from her present
custodians and placed in charge of some person or
persons by whom she shall be more kindly treated.   In
his petition Mr. Bergh states that about six years since
Francis and Mary Connolly, residing at No. 315 West
Forty-first street, obtained possession of the

*Artist's drawing of Officer Christian McDougal carrying
Mary Ellen into the courtroom.*

child from Mr. Kellock, Superintendent of the Department of Charities; that her parents are unknown; that her present custodians have been in the habit of beating her cruelly, the marks of which are now visible on her person; that her punishment was so cruel and frequent as to attract the attention of the residents in the vicinity of the Connolly's dwelling, through whom information of the fact was conveyed to Mr. Bergh; that her custodians had boasted that they had a good fortune for keeping her; that not only was she cruelly beaten, but rigidly confined, and that there was reason to believe that her keepers were about to remove her out of the jurisdiction of the court and beyond the limits of the State.

Upon this petition, Judge Lawrence issued, not an ordinary writ of habeas corpus, but a special warrant, provided for by section 65 of the Habeas Corpus act, whereby the child was at once taken possession of and brought within the control of the court. Under authority of the warrant thus granted, Officer McDougal took the child into custody, and produced her in court yesterday. She is a bright little girl, with features indicating unusual mental capacity, but with a care-worn, stunted, and prematurely old look. Her apparent condition of health, as well as her scanty wardrobe, indicated that no change of custody or condition could be much for the worse.

In his statement of the case to the court, Mr. Elbridge T. Gerry, who appeared as counsel for Mr. Bergh, said the child's condition had been discovered by a lady who had been on an errand of mercy to a dying woman in the house adjoining, the latter asserting that she could not die happy until she had made the child's treatment known; that this statement had been corroborated by several of the neighbors; that the charitable lady who made the discovery of these facts had gone to several institutions in the vain hope of having them take the child under their care; that as a last resort she applied to Mr. Bergh, who, though the case was not within the scope of the special act to prevent cruelty to animals, recognized it as being clearly within the general laws of

Newspaper depiction of Connolly and Mary Ellen. (Courtesy of the George Sim Johnston Archives of the NYSPCC.)

humanity, and promptly gave it his attention. It was urged by council that if the child was not committed to the custody of some proper person, she should be placed in some charitable institution; as, if she was to be returned to her present custodians, it would probably result in her being beaten to death.

The Connollys made no appearance in court, and on her examination the child made a statement as follows: My father and mother are both dead. I don't know how old I am. I have no recollection of a time when I did not live with the Connollys. I call Mrs. Connolly mamma. I have never had but one pair of shoes, but I cannot recollect when that was. I have had no shoes or stockings on this Winter. I have never been allowed to go out of the room where the Connollys were, except in the night time, and then only in the yard. I have never had on a particle of flannel. My bed at night has been only a piece of carpet stretched on the floor underneath a window, and I sleep in my little under-garments, with a quilt over me. I am never allowed to play with any children, or to have any company whatever. Mamma (Mrs. Connolly) has been in the habit of whipping and beating me almost every day. She used to whip me with a twisted whip – a raw hide. The whip always left a black and blue mark on my body. I have now the black and blue marks on my head which were made by mamma, and also a cut on the left side of my head which was made by a pair of scissors. (Scissors produced in court.) She struck me with the scissors and cut me; I have no recollection of ever having been kissed by any one – have never been kissed by mamma. I have never been taken on my mamma's lap and caressed or petted. I never dared to peak to anybody, because if I did I would get whipped. I have never had, to my recollection, any more clothing than I have at present – a calico dress and skirt. I have seen stockings and other clothes in our room, but was not allowed to put them on. Whenever mamma went out, I was locked up in the bedroom. I do not know for what I was whipped – mamma never said anything to me when she whipped me. I do not want to go back to live with mamma, because she beats me so. I have no recollection of ever being on the street in my life.

At this point of the investigation, an adjournment was taken until 10 o'clock A.M. today.

In addition to the forgoing testimony, Messrs. Gerry and Ambrose Monell, counsel on behalf of the application, stated in court that further evidence would be produced corroborating the statement of the child as to the cruelty and neglect which she has sustained; also, as to the mysterious visits of parties to the house of the Connollys, which, taken together with the intelligent and rather refined appearance of the child, tends to the conclusion that she is the child of parents of some prominence in society, who, for some reason, have abandoned her to her present undeserved fate.

Before adjournment the child was removed into the Judge's private room, where, apart from all parties to the proceedings, she corroborated before Judge Lawrence her statement as herein given. Counsel on behalf of Mr. Bergh, in his statement to the court, desired it to be clearly understood that the latter's action in the case has been prompted by his feelings and duty as a humane citizen; that in no sense has he acted in his official capacity as President of the Society for the Prevention of Cruelty to Animals, but is none the less determined to avail himself of such means as the laws place within his power, to prevent the too frequent cruelties practiced on children.

New York Herald, April 10, 1874

THE COURTS

The Heartrending Story of Mary Ellen McCormack – The Philanthropist Bergh to the Rescue

There are few more touching recitals in the English language than Dickens' story of Little Nell, in the "Old Curiosity Shop"; and yet, with all the magnetic power of pathetic fiction infused into the narrative by the transcendent genius of the great novelist, there are at times revealed in our courts incidents from real life greatly surpassing in their touching details the farthest reach of imagination. The trouble is, they are not often brought to light, but, in the mighty, sweeping undercurrent of the busy, bustling life of a great city like ours, flow on with the swelling human tide into the broad ocean of the unfathomable and the unknown. Occasionally a waif floats to the surface and kindly, angelic hands take it in charge, and the story of its sufferings and wrongs is then made known. In Supreme Court Chambers yesterday morning, but little heed was paid to the keenly subtle arguments of lawyers upon motions and counter motions being heard by Judge Lawrence. The attention of nearly every one was directed to a singular group in the rear of the courtroom – a group worthy of the pencil of a Reubens or the sculptured marble of a Powers. Its central figure was a little girl seated in a chair and holding about her a lap robe. Her face was pale and the features molded into lines of rare and exquisite beauty. Such eyes are rarely seen in a child – so large, so dark and so wondering in their expression. In every lineament of the face could be read suffering, and its infantile freshness was marred by marks of fresh cuts and bruises; but as she smiled and with her tiny hands smoothed back from her forehead her wealth of brown hair one almost forgot these and the feeling of roused indignation burning within at thought of possible cruelty to one so young and fair and fragile. As she smiled she looked, indeed, "a thing of beauty, a joy forever." By her side sat Bergh, the one and only Bergh, he of humanitarian fame. A noble enthusiasm seemed to fill his soul, a nobler fire to kindle in his eye. Majestic as he always is, he looked more majestic than ever. The energy of a greater future, moreover, threw a seeming halo about his brow. His thoughts had taken a higher flight, a grander purpose inspired him. He looked the ideal of benevolent heroism. Anyone could see that within that brain was being wrought out a problem farther reaching than horses and cats and dogs and pigeon shooting and cock fighting and rat pits. Directly in front of him was his counsel, Mr. Gerry. His face did not wear the stereotype, hard, legal look. He had a look that meant business. The next prominent figure in the group was a middle-aged lady, dressed in black, but a sweet and tender expression maligning her features – just such a face as one would look for in army hospitals and cities besieged by pestilence. Three officers completed the group – Detectives Dusenbury and McDougal, of Police Headquarters, and Officer Evans, attached to the Society for the Prevention of Cruelty to Animals.

"What means all this?" several asked Mr. Gerry.

"Something that will make your blood boil when you hear the facts," was all that could be elicited from him. This sharpened all the more the general curiosity, but the crowd in attendance did not have to wait long before the facts were made known.

MEANING OF THE GROUP EXPLAINED

Seizing the first opportunity, Mr. Gerry advanced to the railing in front of the Judge's bench and announced how, pursuant to a writ granted by His Honor, he had brought the little girl into court, the barbarous treatment of whom was recited in the petition of Mr. Bergh. He then went on to explain how Mrs. Charles C. Wheeler, having gone to visit a dying woman on the upper floor of the rear tenement house No. 315 West Forty-first street, the latter called attention to frequently hearing the most agonizing shrieks from a child being beaten in an adjoining room, and that she could not die in peace and know that this child was subjected to such torture without something being done to put a stop to it. He then explained further that Mrs. Wheeler inquired among the neighbors and found that Francis and Mary Connolly, with whom the child lived, had said she was not their child; that that the child had been habitually locked in their room, had been beaten cruelly, had been left without shoes or stockings and almost without clothing during the entire winter; that she was troubled about the child and asked advice of many who had no advice to give, till she came to Henry Bergh, who, not as President of the Society, but as a citizen, had at once taken up the cause and made petition, in a somewhat, in a somewhat unusual proceeding for the Court, to inquire as to a proper custodian for the child.

"Are Francis and Mary Connolly in Court?" asked Judge Lawrence.

"They are not," answered Mr. Gerry. "I did not think it necessary to have them here at this stage of the proceeding."

"Should not the parents of the child be notified?" suggested the judge.

"From what I have been able to learn," replied Mr. Gerry, "it is evident that the parents do not wish to be known. Mr. Kellock, of the Commissioners of Charities and Correction Bureau, placed the child with these people some years ago."

"Testimony will have to be taken in the case," said Judge Lawrence, "to verify the allegations set forth in Mr. Bergh's petition."

"I have present only Mrs. Wheeler and the child," answered Mr. Gerry, "and I ask that both be sworn."

MYSTERIES AND MISERIES OF THE METROPOLIS

The little girl was now carried by Officer Evans up to the Judge for him to examine into her fitness to be sworn. As the laprobe was removed and the wee waif, so slender and delicate and with no shoes or stockings on, and only a scant and ragged calico dress and chemise to cover her nakedness and marks of bruises covering her tender limbs, stood by the Judge's side, a thrill of horror and indignation filled the breast of every beholder. The Judge examined her at some length, putting his questions in a low and inaudible voice. "I find her unusually bright," said the Judge; "but through lack of religious teaching, she does not understand the nature of an oath, and I cannot swear her."

THE CHILD'S STATEMENT

Having adjourned to an adjoining room, the child's unsworn statement was taken down as follows: "My name is Mary Ellen McCormack. I don't know how old I am; My mother and father are both dead; I have no recollection of a time when I did not live with the Connollys; I call Mrs. Connolly mama; I have never had but one pair of shoes, but can't recollect when that was. I have had no shoes or stockings on this winter; I have never been allowed to go out of the rooms where the Connollys live except in the nighttime, and then only in the yard; I have never had on a particle of flannel. My bed at night is only a piece of carpet, stretched on the floor underneath a window, and I sleep in my little undergarment, with a quilt over me. I am never allowed to play with any children or have any company whatever. Mama has been in the habit of whipping and beating me almost every day. She used to whip me with a twisted whip, a raw hide. The whip always left black and blue marks on my body. I have now on my head two black and blue marks which were made by mama with the whip, and a cut on the left side of my forehead which was made by a pair of scissors in mama's hand. She struck me with the scissors and cut me. I have no recollection of ever having been kissed, and have never been kissed by mama. I have never been taken on my Mama's lap, or caressed or petted. I never dared to speak to anybody, because if I did I would get whipped; I never had, to my recollection, any more clothing than I have on at present, a calico dress and skirt; I have seen stockings and other clothes in our room, but I am not allowed to put them on; whenever mama went out I was locked up in the bedroom; the scissors with which mama struck me are those now shown by Mr. Evans; I don't know for what I was whipped; mama never said anything to me when she whipped me; I do not want to go back to live with mama, because she beats me so; I have no recollection of ever being in the street in my life."

THOROUGH EXAMINATION OF THE CASE

The examination was here adjourned till this morning, the child meantime being committed to the care of the matron at police Headquarters. Subpoenas were issued for the attendance of Mr. And Mrs. Connolly, and altogether Mr. Gerry says he has some dozen witnesses to examine, and he proposes to make it searching and thorough, and hopes by visiting punishment upon the alleged guilty parties to let others having the custody of children left in their care know that they can be held accountable for the treatment they give them. The detectives say Mrs. Connolly was very abusive when they went after the child. They asked for all the child's clothing, and all she gave them was another worn out calico dress and shredded chemise, which they brought with them and which were exhibited in Court.

New York Daily Tribune, Friday, April 10, 1874

A Case For Charitable Interference – Henry Bergh Rescues A Little Girl From Her Inhuman Parents – Proceedings In The Supreme Court

111

A melancholy and pitiful spectacle formed a pathetic incident in yesterday's proceedings in the Supreme Court, in which a child, terribly abused by its pseudo parents, was rescued and taken before Judge Lawrence for relief. Elbridge T. Gerry and Ambrose Monell, well-known lawyers in this city, appeared before Judge Lawrence day before yesterday in the case entitled "In the matter of the custody of the child called Mary Ellen," and presented the following petition from Henry Bergh:

The petition of Henry Bergh respectfully shows that a little girl, age about 7 years and called Mary Ellen, is held in illegal confinement and custody by a man and woman named Connolly, at and within the premises No. 315 West Forty-first Street, in the City of New York; that said child is not the child of said man and said woman or either of them, nor are they its lawful guardians or entitled to its custody; that such child is now kept in rigid confinement within said premises by the said man and woman, and is unlawfully and illegally restrained of its liberty, and is sad, has been by them daily, and frequently during each day, severely whipped, beaten, struck, and bruised, without any provocation or cause therefore; and that the marks of said beatings and bruises will appear plainly visible upon the body and limbs of the child at the present time upon inspection thereof; that such child has been kept without shoes or stockings during the entire winter; and that the said man and woman have been for a long time past in the constant and usual habit of leaving the child alone locked up in said premises and allowed to remain there crying for a long time, without any other person whatever therein.

Deponent further states that he has received information from those who reside immediately adjacent to said premises, and in the house in which the child is confined, and whom deponent is ready to produce as witnesses to substantiate the statement by him herein above made, that the said man and woman have repeatedly stated that they had a good fortune for keeping the child, and keep her they would, whatever trouble might be made about it, and that such child was not the child of either of them.

Deponent further saith that the said man and woman have resided only recently in the premises in question, and that he is informed and is able to show by the persons aforesaid, and deponent verily believes, that the said man and woman will carry out of the State, or inflict upon the child aforesaid, or that such child will suffer some irreparable injury, and be further cruelly beaten, and, perhaps maimed, by the said man and woman, before such child can be relieved by the issuing of a Habeas corpus or certiorari.

Your petitioner, therefore, prays that a warrant may be immediately issued, pursuant to the statute in such case made and provided, and directed to such sheriff, constable, or other person as it may be deemed proper, and commanding such officer or person to take such child and forthwith to bring her before you to be dealt with according to law. And further, to arrest and bring before you the said man and woman having such child in his, her, or their custody, to be dealt with according to law, pursuant to the statute in such case made and provided.

On this petition Judge Lawrence promptly granted a special warrant for seizing the child and bring it before him, for fear that the man and woman might remove it out of his jurisdiction, granting the warrant under section 65 of the Habeas Corpus act – an unusual warrant to grant. The writ was made returnable yesterday, and accordingly in the morning Detectives McDougal and Dusenbury of the Central Office, accompanied by Officer Evans of the Society for the Prevention of Cruelty to Animals, went to the house and forcibly took the little girl and conveyed her to the court-room of Judge Lawrence.

While Mr. Monell was eliciting from the little waif the story of her wretched life, a crowd gathered and formed a ring of sympathizing listeners. The little girl appeared stunted in growth, was dressed in a thin, threadbare, red-striped calico dress, low in the neck and not reaching to her knees. Under this she had one cotton undergarment, no stockings, no shoes, and no hat. Over this apology for a dress the officers had thrown a lap-robe, and from this, this little pinched white face stretched out, and the small brown eyes peered forth in wonder at such unwonted tenderness. The hands and feet, large and rugged, showed the plain marks of great exposure. She seemed an unusually intelligent child, taking into consideration her unhappy lack of opportunities, and her smile, as she turned to her charitable friend, Mrs. Wheeler, and thanked her for the bread and cake she was eating, was pleasing and childlike, despite the characteristic "old" expression. Her statement, as given to the lawyers, and partially in their language, was as follows:

"My name is Mary Ellen McCormack. I don't know how old I am; My mother and father are both dead; I have no recollection of a time when I did not live with the Connollys; I call Mrs. Connolly mama; I have never had but one pair of shoes, but can't recollect when that was. I have had no shoes or stockings on this winter; I have never been allowed to go out of the rooms where the Connollys live except in the nighttime, and then only in the yard; I have never had on a particle of flannel. My bed at night is only a piece of carpet, stretched on the floor underneath a window, and I sleep in my little undergarment, with a quilt over me. I am never allowed to play with any children or have any company whatever. Mama has been in the habit of whipping and beating me almost every day. She used to whip me with a twisted whip, a raw hide. The whip always left black and blue marks on my body. I have now on my head two black and blue marks which were made by mama with the whip, and a cut on the left side of my forehead which was made by a pair of scissors in mama's hand. She struck me with the scissors and cut me. I have no recollection of ever having been kissed, and have never been kissed by mama. I have never been taken on my Mama's lap, or caressed or petted. I never dared to speak to anybody, because if I did I would get whipped; I never had, to my recollection, any more clothing than I have on at present, a calico dress and skirt; I have seen stockings and other clothes in our room, but I am not allowed to put them on; whenever

115

mama went out I was locked up in the bedroom; the scissors with which mama struck me are those now shown by Mr. Evans; I don't know for what I was whipped; mama never said anything to me when she whipped me; I do not want to go back to live with mama, because she beats me so; I have no recollection of ever being in the street in my life."

The matter will come up again to-day, and some interesting testimony is expected. It is thought that the girl is the illegitimate child of respectable parents, and great efforts will be made to find the truth.

6

Press Coverage, April 11

New York Times, April 11, 1874

THE MISSION OF HUMANITY
Continuation of the Proceedings Instituted by Mr.
Bergh on Behalf of the Child, Mary Ellen Wilson

Proceedings in the case of Mary Ellen Wilson, the
little girl of eight years, charged to have been
cruelly treated by Francis and Mary Connolly, of
No. 315 West Forty-first street, an account of which
appeared in The Times of yesterday, were
continued yesterday, before Judge Lawrence, in
Supreme Court, Chambers. Quite a number of
persons, including several ladies, were attracted to
the court by the publicity which had been given to
the proceedings had on the previous day, all of
them evidently deeply sympathizing with the little
neglected waif, whose cause had been espoused by
Mr. Bergh. Ten o'clock in the morning, to which
the hearing had been adjourned, found the little

girl, Mr. Bergh and his counsel, Messrs. Elbridge T. Gerry and Ambrose Monell, and Mrs. Connolly, the former custodian of the girl, all present in court. The first witness put upon the stand was Mrs. Connolly, who testified as follows: I was formerly married to Thomas McCormack, and had three children by him, all of whom are dead. After Mr. McCormack's death, I married Francis Connolly. Before my first husband died, he had told me he had three children by another woman, who was alive, but was a good-for-nothing. I went with McCormack to Mr. Kellock, and got out the child, Mary Ellen, my husband signing the paper.

Here the paper referred to was produced, and which proved to be an "indenture" of the child, Mary Ellen Wilson, aged one year and six months, to Thomas McCormack, butcher, and his wife, Mary, in February, 1866, and whereby they undertook to report once a year the condition of the child to the commissioners of Charities and Correction. This indenture was endorsed by Commissioner Isaac Bell and Secretary Brown.

Witness continued as follows: I know this was one of my husband's illegitimate children. He selected this one. The mother's name, I suppose, is Wilson, because Mr. Kellock, the Superintendent, had the name down. Mr. Kellock asked no questions about my relation to the child. I told him I wanted this child. My husband never told me where the woman Wilson lived. We got the child out on the 2d of January, without any paper being served or any receipt for the child. This was the only paper we signed, and it was not signed until the 15th of February. Sometimes my husband told me the mother of the child lived down town. I learned from several people who knew my husband that the woman is still alive. I could not tell who they were. They were laborers who came from work with him and stopped there drinking. I have no way of knowing if the woman is still alive, or if she has any relatives. I never received a cent for supporting this child. At the time I took the child we were living at No. 866 Third avenue, and my husband said the mother left it there, and he would take it out until such time as she called for it. I have instructed the child according to the undertaking in the indenture – that there is a God, and what it is to lie. I have not instructed her in "the art and mystery of housekeeping," because she is too young. She had a flannel petticoat when she came to me, and I gave her no others.

At this point the witness grew somewhat excited at Mr. Gerry, the examining counsel, whom she assumed to be ignorant of the difficulties of bringing up and governing children, and concluded her testimony by an admission that on but two occasions had she complied with the conditions of the indenture requiring her to report once a year to the Commissioners of Charities and Correction the condition of the child.

New York Herald, April 11, 1874

THE COURTS

The Child Cruelty Case
Further Examination of Witnesses
More Of The Little Waif, It's Brief and Sad Life History, As Told By Various Witnesses

Mrs. Connolly, The Step-Mother, In Lieu Of
Explanation, Lectures Counsel

Attracted no doubt by the account given in the
Herald of the sad young life of the little waif, Mary
Ellen McCormack, there was a large crowd,
including a number of ladies, present at the further
examination in the case had yesterday in the court
room of Oyer and Terminer. The young girl, Mary,
a novel experience in her young career, was "the
observed of all observers." She looked as
childishly simple and sweet as when first brought
into court, though still clad in the same scant
habiliments of wretched poverty and with the
marks of the barbarous cruelty to which she has
been subjected still visible upon her face. The next
object of interest was Mrs. Connolly, against whom
these cruelties are charged. She is a middle-aged
woman, of a spare figure and not altogether
unprepossessing countenance, and certainly does
not look to be the inhuman monster she is
represented as being. Bergh, the great hater of
cruelty in all its forms, who has invoked the law to
rescue this waif from her life of hardship and
persecution, was promptly on hand, and so were
his counsel, Messrs. Gerry and Monell.
Considerable testimony was taken, all the material
points of which will be found in the subjoined
report of the day's proceedings:

MRS. CONNOLLY TELLS HER STORY.
The first witness called was Mrs. Connolly. She
stated that she resided at present on the upper back
floor of the rear tenement house No. 315 West
Forty-first street; in 1851 she married Mr.

McCormack and had three children by him, who all are dead; after McCormack's death she married Francis Connolly; before her first husband died he told her frequently he had three children by another woman, who was alive, but was a good for nothing; she understood from her first husband that Mary Ellen was his child; sometimes he would say she was, sometimes that she was not; that was somewhere about 1855; my second marriage was in 1867; my first husband died in 1866; I received the child about 1867; after my husband died I understood he had three children; I have a paper which I want you to look at; here it is.

INDENTURE OF THE CHILD
Mr. Gerry read a paper given him by the witness, describing the child as Mary Ellen Wilson; it contains the old formal provisions of indenture under the common law, and the special provisions under the statutes of New York; they are dated February 6, 1866, and substantially provide for an "adoption" with provisions for the good treatment and education of the child.

MRS. CONNOLLY CONTINUES
My first husband told me she was his illegitimate child; well I believed him, of course; the mother's name, I suppose, is Wilson, because Mr. Kellock asked no questions about my connection with the child, and my husband never told me where the woman Wilson lived; we got the child out on the 2d of January, without any paper being served or any receipt for the child; this was the only paper we signed; it was not signed until the 15th of February; sometimes my husband told me the

mother of the child lived down town; I learned from several people who knew my husband that the woman is still alive; I couldn't tell who they were; they were laborers that came from work with him and stopped there drinking; I have no way of knowing whether the woman is alive and whether she has any relatives; I never received a cent for supporting the child; I was living at No. 866 Third avenue when we took out the child, and my husband said the mother left it there and he would take it out until such time as she called for it; I have instructed the child, according to the undertaking in the indenture, that there is a God; I told her what a lie is; I haven't instructed her in "the art and mystery of housekeeping", because she is too young; she had a flannel petticoat when she came to me; I did give her others.

SHE GETS VERY EXCITED

"But you see that the child has on (Mary Ellen standing up) a fragment of a calico dress," continued Mr. Gerry, going on with the examination, "and a little worn out chemise under it and no shoes or stockings or bonnet, and these, with another shredded dress and chemise, were, you told the officers, all her clothes. Do you call this dressing her well?"

"This whole thing is a persecution," answered Mrs. Connolly. "And got up by people who do not know what they are about."

"You will find by and by whether they know anything about it," mildly responded Mr. Gerry.

"So you say," spoke up Mrs. Connolly in a savagely irate tone, and in a very excited manner and with great volubility she gave Mr. Gerry her ideas of the duties of parents to children and the difficulty of bringing them up. It was with some difficulty she could be induced to stop talking.

THE CHILD CROUCHING IN A CORNER

Alonzo S. Evans, an officer of the Society for the Prevention of Cruelty to Animals, was the next witness examined. He testified that when he called to the house of last witness, the child was crouching in a corner, and lifted up its hands as if fearing a blow; Mrs. Connolly said the child was not hers; the child had no clothing but what it has on now; Officer McDougal got a rug and put it around the child, and carried it to Superintendent Matsell's office; after the witness and Officers McDougal and Dusenbury went back to demand the child's wardrobe, Mrs. Connolly handed out the few articles now produced; while in Mr. Matsell's office, the child stated the cuts on her face were made by Mrs. Connolly with the scissors now produced; while the officers were getting the child's wardrobe and the scissors they also searched for the cowhide known to be there, but couldn't find it; Mrs. Connolly was very abusive and used an expression which he considered obscene; while they were taking away the child in a carriage, it was very nervous and timorous; the child told them Mrs. Connolly whipped her every morning with a raw cowhide and showed marks on her body. During his second conversation with Mrs. Connolly, she told him that Mr. Kellock's head clerk quietly said to her he knew the mother of the child, but he wouldn't tell her.

STORY OF TWO DETECTIVES

Detective McDougal, of Police Headquarters, confirmed Mr. Evans' story as to the child's condition and story, giving the child's story in somewhat more dramatic form; he also confirmed Mr. Evans' statement as to Mrs. Connolly's behavior and obscene language; he added that the child told him in the carriage that her mama struck her with the scissors for not holding a cloth properly, and that she was in the habit of whipping her with a cowhide.

Officer Dusenbury, in addition to telling the same story, testified that when he asked Mrs. Connolly for the child's clothes, she said that the two articles produced were her only wardrobe; she said when she got her back she would whip her as she had before.

A NEIGHBOR'S TESTIMONY

Mrs. Charlotte Hergeling, a German, who lives at No. 325 West Forty-first Street, testified that Mrs. Connolly lived in the same house with her some months ago; she never actually saw Mrs. Connolly beat the child, but she often heard the child crying; one very cold day she saw the child go into the yard with nothing on but a petticoat; she asked the child why she did not put on shoes and stockings and the child said she daren't, her mama wouldn't let her; one side of the child's body was all black and blue with whipping marks; she spoke to Mrs. Connolly and Mrs. Connolly said anyone who interfered would have to go to the highest law.

THE CHILD A PRISONER

Mrs. Kemp, who lived at No. 325 West Forty-first Street for two years while Mrs. Connolly lived there, testified that the child was kept in close confinement all this time in a back room; the child always trembled when Mrs. Connolly came home; she used to be locked into the little room all day.

HEARING BLOWS

Mary Studor, a resident of No. 323 West Forty-first Street, next door to the Connollys, had never even seen the child but very frequently she heard her crying, and very frequently heard blows; not every day, but very often.

ALWAYS LOCKED IN

Mrs. Margaret Bingham, who lives in No. 325 West Forty-first Street, testified that she let rooms in the rear to Mrs. Connolly, who told her she had one child; the child wore an apron and a little petticoat like that on her that "done her no good". This was two years ago; after some time they began to wonder where the child was, always locked in and the windows down; she told the neighbors, and they said it was no use to interfere, as the police wouldn't listen to her, and witness knew nothing about this cruelty to animals. Witness went on to tell how they tried to open the window where the child was confined, and could only get it up one inch; the child had a cut on her chin once; Mrs. Connolly kept the cowhide in the back room; Mrs. Connolly used to go out and remain out all day,

125

leaving the child locked in the back room; she never once took the child out; she once told witness that the husband was trying to get the child into an asylum but "I got a good fortune with the child to keep it," says she, "and I mean to keep it."

WHIPPED EVERY MORNING
Charles Smith, whose wife's dying condition first attracted Mrs. Wheeler to the house, testified that almost every morning he heard blows falling on the child and the child crying; that was just after Mr. Connolly went to work; the whipping lasted about a quarter of an hour.

AFRAID OF CONTAMINATION
Mrs. Slater, Mrs. Bingham's daughter, testified that during the hot summer two years ago, the Connollys' rooms were so persistently shut up that she could not believe there was any child in them, but afterwards she saw the child at the window; then the Connollys put catches on the blinds so that the child could not open them; she saw the child once out in the yard, and once or twice besides; once it had shoes on and once, besides its present dress, a little apron; Mrs. Connolly, when she suggested that the child be allowed to play with her own little girl, said she did not want her contaminated by other children.

A RAWHIDE ON THE TABLE
Mrs. Charles G. Wheeler told how she went to Mrs. Smith and tried to get Mrs. Connolly to let the little girl go in and attend on Mrs. Smith. When she first went in Mrs. Connolly's room she found the child standing up on a keg washing dishes; there was a

rawhide lying on the table; the child took no notice of her; Mrs. Connolly have an evasive answer; on her next visit to Mrs. Connolly for the same purpose the child was sitting down, and the rawhide on a chair near her; in passing on her visits to Mrs. Smith the door of the Connolly's room was sometimes open, but was at once closed; she saw the child several times, sometimes on the bitterest days of winter; she saw her dress, and except once, when she had a little slip on, it was the same as she now had; she never saw her wearing either shoes or stockings; the Connolly's blinds were always down.

The further examination of witnesses was here adjourned till this morning.

New York Daily Tribune, April 11, 1874

A CHILD'S SUFFERINGS
Mr. Bergh's Protégé in Court Again – The Story of Mary Ellen's Step-Mother

The proceedings which began on Thursday in Supreme Court Chambers before Judge Lawrence for the rescue of the little girl Mary Ellen from the violence of its step-mother, Mary Connolly, were continued yesterday. The object of this practical sympathy, wrapped in the lap-robe with which the officers had covered her, was surrounded by the ladies and gentlemen who had made her cause their own; among them Mrs. C.G. Wheeler and two friends, Mr. Bergh and Messrs. Gerry and Monell, her counsel. The child seemed to have lost some of her feeling of fear and chatted with her protectors, her small, pinched face lighting up at their expressions of kindness. It is said that Mrs. Wheeler, after investigating the case thoroughly, found it very difficult to interest any one in behalf of the child until she met Mr. Bergh.

The first witness examined was Mary Connolly, the woman who is accused of brutally beating Mary Ellen. She gave her testimony with great volubility and was at one time very abusive in her language to Mr. Gerry. She is apparently about 38 years old, with a sharp, hardened face. She said that she was formerly married to Thomas McCormack and she had understood from him that she was his child, although he made contradictory statements about it. He died in 1866, and she married Francis Connolly in 1867. Before her first husband died, he told her frequently he had three children by another woman, and that the woman was alive. McCormack and witness went to the office of George Kellock and secured the child Mary Ellen, her husband signing the necessary papers. Here the witness produced a paper which was the indenture of the child, Mary Ellen Wilson, aged one year and six months, to Thomas McCormack, butcher, and his wife Mary, dated Feb 6, 1866, they undertaking to report the condition of the child once a year to the Commissioners of Charities and Correction. The indenture was endorsed by Commissioner Isaac Bell and Isaac Bowen, Secretary. The usual provisions in regard to good treatment and education were inserted. The witness continued as follows: I knew this was one of my husband's illegitimate children; The mother's name, I suppose, is Wilson, because Mr. Kellock, the Superintendent of Out Door Poor had the name down; Mr. Kellock asked no questions about my connection with the child; I told him I wanted this child out; the other two were a girl and boy; my husband never told me where the woman Wilson lived; sometimes he told me she lived out of the city, and sometimes he said she lived in New York; we received the child on Jan. 2 without any paper being signed or any receipt given for the child; this was the only paper we signed and it was not signed until Feb. 15; I learned from several people who knew my husband that the woman is still alive; I couldn't tell who they were; they were laborers that came from work with him and stopped there drinking; I have no way of knowing whether the woman is alive, and whether she has any relative; I never received a cent for supporting the child; I was living at No. 866 Third Ave. when we took out the child; my husband said the mother left it there, and he would take it out until such time as she called for it; I have instructed the child, according to the undertaking of the indenture, that there is a God; I told her what a lie is; I did not teach her housekeeping because she is too young; I took her twice to see the commissioners of charities and correction, but they did not seem to care, so I didn't take her again; She had flannel undergarments when she came to me, and I gave her the others.

The witness became very excited when questioned in regard to the child's clothing, and very volubly denounced the proceedings as meddlesome and interference by people who do not know what they were doing.   Alonzo S. Evans, an officer of Mr.

Bergh's society, and officers McDougal and Dusenbury, who took the child from Mrs. Connolly, testified to the child's condition when taken. She was timid and frightened, and told them how she had been whipped and stuck with a pair of scissors. The woman was reticent about the child, and used abusive and obscene language with them, and threatened to whip the child when she was returned to her. Mrs. Charlotte Heigling, who lived in the same house with the Connollys, testified that she had seen the child in the yard in the coldest weather with nothing on except a light thin petticoat; she spoke to the girl, and she answered that she didn't dare to put anything on for fear her "mama" would beat her; she was then black and blue from whipping. Other witnesses testified to the evident fear which the girl felt toward this woman, the sounds of blows and crying which they had heard, and her imprisonment and seclusion. One witness attested that Mrs. Connolly said that her husband wanted her to get rid of the child, but she had a good fortune to take care of the child and she was going to do it.

The case was adjourned until 10:30 AM today, the child being remanded to the care of the officers.

Buffalo Daily Courier, Saturday Morning, April 11, 1874

FEARFUL CRUELTY TO A CHILD

The Miseries of an Orphan in New York – A sad Tale in the Court of Oyer and Terminer – Mr. Bergh's Good Work.

New York Evening Post, April 9.

A little girl, barefooted and bareheaded, apparently about eight years of age, but with that tightened skin which gives the appearance of greater age, was brought yesterday before Mr. Justice Lawrence, wrapped in a rug to give her the protection which her ragged and scanty garments did not afford.

Mr. Gerry, appearing for the little waif, stated that Mrs. Charles C. Wheeler, being on an errand of mercy to a dying woman in 315 West Forty-first street, heard the suffering of a child near, and the dying woman said that she could not die in peace while the child was so suffering. Mrs. Wheeler inquired among the neighbors and found that Francis and Mary Connolly, with whom the child lived, had said she was not their child; that the child had been habitually locked in their room, had been beaten cruelly, and had been left without shoes or stockings and almost without clothing during the entire winter; that she was troubled about the child, and asked advice of many who had no advice to give till she came to Henry Bergh, who, not as president of the society but as a citizen, had at once taken up the cause. He had made petition, in a somewhat unusual proceeding for the court, to inquire as to a proper custodian for the child.

Judge Lawrence yesterday granted a writ to bring the child before him, and the police this morning brought down the child, who bore the marks on her face of a blow from a large pair of scissors.

Francis and Mary Connolly were called, but did not answer.

Judge Lawrence asked whether the parents of the child should not be notified.

Mr. Gerry answered that from what he had been able to ascertain, it seemed that the parents did not wish to be known. Mr. Kellogg had placed the child with these people some years ago.

Judge Lawrence suggested that testimony must be taken.

Mr. Gerry had present only Mrs. Wheeler and the child, and asked that both be sworn. The little child was taken up to Judge Lawrence, who examined her at some length, but though unusually bright, Judge Lawrence had to refuse to swear her, because of her lack of religious teaching.

Mr. Gerry asked that pending the necessary examination she be committed to some one of half a dozen people he would name. The proceeding – not the usual one – had been taken under the fear that under the ordinary writ, she would be hurried away by her custodians and had been executed very promptly by the detective police.

Judge Lawrence directed that for the present [remainder illegible].

7

Press Coverage, April 12 – April 14

New York Herald, April 12, 1874

THE COURTS

The Little Cinderella, Mary Ellen McCormack –
Good Fairy Bergh's Development
More About The Little Waif

STATEMENT OF THE DYING WOMAN WHO
COULD NOT DIE IN PEACE UNTIL THE CHILD
WAS RESCUED FROM HER TORMENTORS –
GROWING PUBLIC INTEREST IN THE CASE

The case of the little child, Mary Ellen McCormack,
has evidently excited a wide spread feeling of
interest in her behalf. Already a number of ladies,

whose sympathies have been moved by the painful recitals of the barbarous cruelties inflicted upon her by her inhuman stepmother and whose benevolent impulses have also, doubtless, been additionally stirred by the exceeding sprightliness and beauty of the little waif, have already offered to take care of her. As Mr. Gerry, who with Mr. Ambrose Monell, is acting as counsels for Mr. Bergh in the case, came into the court room of the Court of Oyer and Terminer yesterday, where the examination was to be resumed, a letter was handed him from a leading merchant of the city offering to adopt the child. And this young life, so crushed and trampled upon in the bud, is likely, after all, to blossom into brightness and beauty.

STORY OF A DYING WOMAN

The only additional evidence yesterday was submitting the statement of Mrs. Mary Smith who lives in an apartment adjoining that of Francis and Mary Connolly, on the top floor of the rear tenement house, No. 315 West Forty-first Street. This is the woman whom Mrs. Wheeler called to see, learning that she was very sick and not likely to recover, and to whose statement regarding the ill treatment of the child and that she could not die in peace unless something was done to rescue her from the cruelties to which she was subjected is due the present investigation. Her statement begins by saying that she is a dying woman, and has been given up by eight doctors.

"No woman could possibly survive eight doctors," broke in Mr. Gerry at this point of the reading with what some might consider rather ill-timed jocoseness, and he and others laughed as though he had said a good thing.

"It would, indeed, be a marvelous miracle," added Mr. Bergh, in a tone of most sepulchral gravity, for, like the bard who is saddest when he sings, his countenance is never so preternaturally elongated as when he essays a humorous vein.

But to go on with the statement of the dying woman. She continued by stating that the Connollys came to live there four months ago and brought the child Mary Ellen with them. She heard Mrs. Connolly "lick" the child every day, mostly in the morning before breakfast, sometimes before the husband went to work, but mostly after it; if she did not lick her in the morning, she licked her during the day; sometimes she licked her twice in the day; when Mrs. Connolly went out you could hardly believe a child was there all the time; once the child came to the door when Mrs. Connolly was out, but on seeing Mrs. Smith she ran back frightened and locked the door.

THE COWHIDE

During the first week after the Connollys came there witness saw the cowhide lying on the table; it is like what a man uses when on horseback; it is about two and a half feet long; it has lashes (she doesn't know how many) about the size of a finger, something like a cat-o-nine-tails; she used to hear Mrs. Connolly licking the child every morning "up and down, up and down" the room, the child crying "Oh, Mama! Mama!" all the time; in conversation with Mrs. Connolly the latter said she never knew such a child; she said it was a little devil, that it knew more than a girl of ten or eleven, and that she couldn't have a bit or a sup unknown to her husband, as the child told him everything; she had seen the child lying in a corner of the room under the window, and believes that was where she slept and passed all her time.

THE CHILD'S ANTECEDENTS

Mr. Gerry here informed Judge Larremore that the Commissioners of Charities and Correction and Mr. George Kellock had undertaken to cause a search to be made in the office for all documents bearing on the case, so as to throw light, if possible, on the child's antecedents. The inquiry was then adjourned to eleven o'clock tomorrow morning.

New York Herald, April 14, 1874

THE COURTS

LITTLE MARY ELLEN MCCORMACK

A Bevy Of Ladies Attend Her In Court – New Clothes For The Waif And New Joy In Her Heart – Her Condition When Taken To Police Headquarters – The Indenture From The Commissioners Of Charities And Correction – Arrest Of Mrs. Connolly

The absorbing case of interest in the courts continues to be that of the little waif, Mary Ellen McCormack. In Supreme Court Chambers, before Judge Lawrence, where the examination was to be resumed yesterday, a large and curious crowd was present and anxious to get a glimpse of this wee bit creature, the recital of whose tiny life history of cruel wrong and persecution has warmed so many generous hearts with sympathy. About a dozen ladies were seated around her, while one held her in her lap. How different she looked from the time she was first brought into court. The scanty and tattered garments she then wore had been replaced by a complete new suit. Comfortable shoes and stockings encased her fairy-like feet. A most becoming little hat sat with bewitching jauntiness on her head, the rich glow of the ribbons enhancing the beauty of her soft brown hair. She looked like a little fairy, her tiny figure so spritelike in its delicate outlines, her large black eyes radiant with joy and an expression of childlike pleasure illuminating every lineament of her expressive face. As she turned over a large picture book and chatted with the ladies she was all smiles and delight. Mr. Bergh was present as usual, his interest in the case seeming to increase as the examination progressed. There was also present with him his counsel, Messrs. E.T. Gerry and Ambrose Monell. Mrs. Connolly appeared in obedience to the direction of the Court for the purpose of signing her deposition. Having done this, she approached little Mary and extended her hand, which the latter eagerly seized. In her present intensity of joy the child forgot all about the bitter past, and said, "Good morning, mama, I have got new clothes."

MARY AFTER THE RESCUE
The taking of further testimony was resumed by first calling to the stand Mrs. Mary Webb. She testified as follows: I am matron at Police

Headquarters; my duty is to take charge of the stray children brought there; I examined the child Mary Ellen after she was placed in my care; her clothing was very bad and very dirty; there were vermin in her hair which appeared as if it had never been combed; her body was very dirty, and three distinct washings were necessary to get rid of the dirt encrusted on her; there was a bruise on her hip and one above the elbow, recently made, and one on the temple which she said was caused by a blow of a whip from her mama; there were scratches on her face, which she said were done with a pair of scissors.

INDENTURING THE CHILD
Mr. George Kellock, Superintendent of Outdoor Poor, in the Department of Charities and Correction, testified in answer to Mr. Gerry, that he looked over the records relating to the child Mary Ellen Wilson in an indenture issued from that office in 1866, and signed by him. He produced a book in which was the following entry:

Mary Ellen Wilson, eighteen months old, left in charge of deponent 21st May, 1864, has received $8 a month until three weeks ago; does not know where the mother lives, as per affidavit of Mary Score, No. 235 Mulberry Street.
July 7, 1865

The date (July 7) was the date of the entry. The affidavit of Mary Score could not be found, but search will be made again; the $8 a month was paid by the person who left the child in charge of Mary Score, and when it was stopped she brought it to the Department of Charities; witness does not know Mary Score; the child was forwarded to the Almshouse on Blackwell's Island until the time when Mrs. McCormack and her husband called for the child and adopted it out; they gave a reference that they were competent persons – a Dr. Loughlin; he thinks he could find where the doctor lives; he believed his recommendation enough, and it never occurred to him the child could be ill-treated until he saw it in the papers; the McCormacks did not say a work about it being an illegitimate child of McCormack's; he has not seen Dr. McLoughlin or McLaughlin since; he thinks he lived near Twenty-third Street and Third Avenue; about 50 children a year pass through the department, and he has no recollection of this one in particular; no one, except Mrs. Connolly and her first husband, ever called about the child or showed any interest in it.

The inquiry was here adjourned until Thursday morning.

ARREST OF MRS. CONNOLLY

Mrs. Connolly was arrested on leaving the Court, on a warrant granted by Judge Brady, and committed to the Tombs to await the action of the Grand Jury on a charge of felonious assault.

New York Times, April 14, 1874

Mr. Geo. Kellock, Superintendent of Outdoor Poor, testified that a child named Mary Ellen Wilson was indentured from the Department of Charities in 1866, being then eighteen months old; that the records show the same to have been left there on the 21st of May, 1864, by a woman named Mary Score, giving her address as No. 235 Mulberry street, and who swore that until within three weeks of that time she had received $8 per month for the child's support; had no means of knowing who the child's parents were, and nothing was said by either Mr. McCormack or his wife, Mrs. Connolly, at the time, as to any relationship of either of them to the child; the $8 per month had been paid to Mary Score by the parties leaving the child with her, and it was when that payment stopped that she brought the child to his office. Reference was demanded from Mr. And Mrs. McCormack when they took the child, and they gave their family physician, Dr. Laughlin or McLaughlin, whose statement in reference to them was deemed satisfactory, and an order for the delivery of the child was given accordingly; believes he can find Dr. Laughlin, who lived in the vicinity of Twenty-third street and Third avenue. During the past year about 500 children have passed through the department, and witness has no recollection of this one other than the records of his office record. At this point the further hearing was adjourned to Thursday morning next, at 10 o'clock A.M.

New York Daily Tribune, April 14, 1874

CRUELTY TO A CHILD
Further Investigation Of The Case Of Mary Ellen
Wilson – Mrs. Connolly Arrested

The famous case of the child, Mary Ellen, who was rescued from the ill-usage of the Connollys by the efforts of Mrs. Charles C. Wheeler and Henry Bergh, was brought up in Supreme Court, Chambers, again yesterday. A dozen ladies were present among the mass of lawyers, to hear the continuation of the examination, and the liveliest interest and sympathy were visible on all faces. The little child would hardly be recognized now, so great a change has been effected in her appearance within the last few days. Yesterday she was clothed in a new suit, and the novelty of it as well as of her new position, surrounded by kindness, seemed to fill out the pale little face, which beamed with delight as the child turned over the pages of her new picture-book, probably the only one she had ever seen, or looked up to chat with the ladies. Mrs. Connolly, the woman against whom the charges of cruelty are preferred, was in the court-room and drew a considerable share of the general attention. She came to sign her deposition, and after this had been done, she stepped up to the child and shook hands with her. The child responded with "Good morning, Mamma," and added, pointing to her dress, "I have got new clothes." She exhibited no fear of Mrs. Connolly, and apparently no strong dislike.

Before any testimony was taken the party went into the Circuit Court room, and then Mrs. Mary Webb, Matron at Police Headquarters, whose duty it is to take charge of the stray children brought in, described the child's condition when she came into her own hands. The clothing was very bad and very dirty. There were vermin in her hair and it required three distinct washings to get rid of the incrusted dirt. There was a bruise on her hip, and one above the elbow, recently made, and one on the temple, which she said was caused by a blow of a whip from her mamma. Those were scratches, done with a pair of scissors.

George Kellock, Superintendent of the Out Door Poor in the Department of Charities and Correction, said he had looked over the records relating to the child called "Mary Ellen Wilson," in an indenture issued from that office in 1866, and signed by him. He produced a book containing the following entry:

"Mary Ellen Wilson months old; left in charge of deponent May 21, 1864: has received $8 per month until three weeks ago; does not know where her mother lives, as per affidavit of Mary Score, No. 235 Mulberry Street."

"July 7, 1865." (Date of entry)

The affidavit of Mary Score has not yet been obtained, but efforts will be made to discover her whereabouts. The item of "$8 per month" refers to the sum paid to Mary Score by the person who left the child in her charge. When the pay ceased she brought the child to the Department of Charities. Mr. Kellock said he did not know Mary Score; and continuing the history of the child, said he sent her to the Almshouse on Blackwell's Island, where she remained until Mrs. Connolly, Mrs. McCormack, and her husband, called there to adopt it, giving as reference in regard to their respectability and competency a Dr. Loughlin. Mr. Kellock said he thought he could find this doctor and would try. He thought he lived on Third-ave., somewhere near Twenty-third-st. The witness added it was impossible for him to recollect more about the child, as about 500 children pass through the Department every year. No one but Mrs. Connolly and her first husband ever called to see the child, or appeared to take any interest in her, and they never hinted that the child was illegitimate. After Mr. Kellock's testimony, the further hearing was adjourned, and as soon as the adjournment was announced, Mrs. Connolly was arrested and committed to the Tombs on a warrant issued by Judge Brady, charging [remainder illegible].

8

Press Coverage: April 22 – December 27

New York Times, April 22, 1874

MARY ELLEN WILSON
Mrs. Connolly, the Guardian, Found Guilty, and
Sentenced One Year's Imprisonment at Hard Labor

Mary Connolly, the discovery of whose inhuman treatment of the little waif, Mary Ellen Wilson, caused such excitement and indignation in the community, was placed on trial before Recorder Hackett yesterday, in the Court of General Sessions. The prisoner, whose appearance is anything but prepossessing, sat immovable during the proceedings, never lifting her eyes from the ground, except when the child was first placed on the stand. Little Mary Ellen, an interesting-looking child, was neatly dressed in the new clothes provided for her by the humane ladies who have taken an interest in her, and has so much improved since her first appearance in the courts as to be

Another artist's depiction of Mary Connolly and Mary Ellen. (Courtesy of the George Sim Johnston Archives of the NYSPCC.)

scarcely recognized as the cowering, half-naked child rescued by Mr. Bergh's officers.

The child was brought into court in charge of Mrs. Webb, the matron at Police Headquarters. Mr. Bergh occupied a seat beside District Attorney Rollins, and took an active part in the proceedings.

145

There were two indictments against the prisoner, one for feloniously assaulting Mary Ellen Wilson with a pair of scissors on the 7th of April, and the other for a series of assaults committed during the years 1873 and 1874. The trial yesterday was on the indictment charging felonious assault.

The little child was put upon the stand, and having been instructed by Recorder Hackett in the nature and responsibility of an oath, was sworn. At first she answered the questions put to her readily, but soon became frightened and gave way to sobs and tears. She was soon reassured, however, by the kind words of the Recorder and District Attorney Rollins, and intelligently detailed the story of her ill-treatment. The scar on her forehead when taken from Mrs. Connolly's house, had been inflicted, she said, by her "mamma" with a pair of scissors. Her "mamma" as she called Mrs. Connolly, had been ripping a quilt, which she held, and struck her with the scissors because she did not like how the quilt was held. The child stated that she had been repeatedly beaten with a long cane by her "mamma" without having done anything wrong. The general cruelty and neglect of Mrs. Connolly were also testified to by the child, as has already been published in the proceedings of the preliminary examinations. Mrs. Webb, Matron at Police Headquarters, Detective McDougall, Alonzo S. Evans, of Mr. Bergh's society, Mrs. Wheeler of St. Luke's Mission, Mrs. Bingham, from whom the prisoner rented apartments, Mrs. Tates, and Charles Smith, testified to the bruises and filth on the child's body when rescued from Mrs. Connolly's and to the instances of ill-treatment which had come to their knowledge. After an able argument from District Attorney Rollins and a charge of characteristic clearness from the Recorder, the jury retired, and after twenty minutes deliberation, returned a verdict of guilt of assault and battery.

Recorder Hackett, addressing the prisoner, said that he had no doubt whatever of her guilt. She had been accorded every opportunity to prove her innocence, and the court was fully satisfied that she had been guilty of gross and wanton cruelty. He would have been satisfied if the jury had found her guilty of the higher offense charged. As a punishment to herself, but more as a warning to others, he would sentence her to the extreme penalty of the law – one year in the Penitentiary at hard labor. The prisoner heard her sentence without moving a muscle, and preserved the same hard, cruel expression of countenance displayed by her during the trial, while being conveyed to the Tombs.

A brother of Mrs. Connolly says that the child was legally adopted by the prisoner, who has the legal proofs in her possession, and will seek to gain the custody of the little one at the expiration of her term of punishment.

New York Herald, April 22, 1874

THE COURTS

The Little Waif Once More

THE CASE OF THE LITTLE WAIF.
TRYING TO SOLVE THE MYSTERY OF HER
BIRTH – AN OFFICER IN WILSON'S ZOUAVES
SAID TO BE THE FATHER

Gradually the shadows surrounding the parentage of little Mary Ellen McCormack are being dispelled. Mr. Bergh, who set the investigation in motion, and his zealous counsel, Messrs. E.T. Gerry and Ambrose Monell, whose enthusiasm in the case is only second to that of the great humanitarian himself, express a determination to leave no stone unturned until the mystery at present surrounding the parentage of this little waif is thoroughly exploited and understood. The further examination in the case was resumed yesterday before Judge Lawrence of the Supreme Court. Little Mary is still the object of general interest, as was shown by the throng gathering about her yesterday after she was brought into court. She is getting more accustomed to her new clothes, but her sweetness of manner and face continues unaltered.

Mary Score was the only witness examined yesterday. She testified that the child was brought to her by a chambermaid in the St. Nicholas Hotel, named Kavanagh, who said it was the child of a

Fanny Wilson; Mrs. Wilson saw her and said her husband had been an officer in "Billy" Wilson's Zouaves; she was offered $2 a week, and took the child; she kept her for about a year and then sought for Fanny Wilson, whom she found at the Soldier's Relief Agency, in Eleventh Street; Mrs. Wilson there turned over to her her ticket for relief; the witness could not remember the name on the relief ticket or just how long she was paid under it; she had simply drawn her money and taken good care of the child while the money was paid, and when it failed had turned it over to the Commissioners of Charities and Correction.

Mr. Gerry cross-examined Mrs. Score at great length as to who Fanny Wilson was, but Mrs. Score knew apparently little more than she had already told. The woman Kavanagh was now dead.

An adjournment then took place till next Monday. Meantime the woman, Mrs. Connolly, who took the child from the Department of Charities, is under arrest for cruel treatment of the child.

"The Tombs" where Connolly was incarcerated.

New York Herald, April 28, 1874

THE COURTS
Court Of General Sessions

TRIAL OF MARY CONNOLLY FOR A CRUEL ASSAULT UPON "LITTLE MARY ELLEN" – SHE IS CONVICTED OF ASSAULT AND BATTERY AND SENT TO THE PENITENTIARY FOR ONE YEAR

BEFORE RECORDER HACKETT

The only case disposed of by the jury in this Court yesterday was an indictment against Mary Connolly for a felonious assault upon Mary Ellen Wilson, a little child, at her apartments, No. 315 West Forty-first Street, which is a rear tenement house. It will be remembered that a lengthy investigation was had this month before Judge Lawrence, in the Supreme Court, Chambers, as to the future custody of the child, who was treated unkindly and cruelly by Mrs. Connolly. The testimony taken then appeared in full in the Herald, and as the evidence given by the witnesses upon the trial of the defendant is substantially the same, only its salient points need be recapitulated now. When the woman was arraigned last week upon the indictment the Recorder assigned Messrs. Howe and Hummell to defend her. There were two indictments found by the Grand Jury against Mary Connolly, and the specific charge upon which she was tried was that, on the 7th of April, she stabbed Mary Ellen Wilson in the forehead with a pair of scissors. To sustain the allegation District Attorney Rollins first called the little girl, who was tastefully dressed and looked more like the petted daughter of wealthy parents than a tenement house "waif". It was with extreme difficulty that Mr. Rollins succeeded in getting her to answer the questions propounded, but the main facts were finally elicited from her – that on some day while the prisoner was working at a quilt she cut her in the forehead with a pair of scissors, and on other occasions she beat her with a cowhide. Mr. Howe objected to the admission of evidence as to acts other than the one mentioned in the indictment.

Mr. Rollins claimed that he had a right to introduce proofs of other acts of violence as tending to rebut a theory which the counsel might possibly set up that the cut with the scissors was accidental. Mrs. Webb, who takes charge of lost children who are brought to the Police Headquarters, stated that when the little girl was received by her she was extremely filthy, bare-footed and thinly dressed; that there was a deep scratch on her head and she had live bruises on her body in the region of the hip. Officer McDougal, to whom was entrusted a warrant for the production of the child, said he was accompanied by Mr. Evans, an officer connected with Mr. Bergh's Society for the Prevention of Cruelty to Animals, and that they took her away from the top floor of this tenement house to the headquarters of the police, and returned for the purpose of getting a cowhide which they supposed was there, but they could not find it. Mrs. Wheeler, a lady who was engaged in dispensing the charities of St. Luke's Mission, stated that she visited the tenement house in which the prisoner resided frequently during the months of December, January and February, for the purpose of ministering to a sick woman who occupied a room next to Mrs. Connolly; that upon the first visit to Mrs. Connolly's apartment the little girl was washing dishes, and upon the table nearby she noticed a large cowhide made of strips of leather compactly twisted together, large at one end and tapering at the other. The witness asked Mrs. Connolly if she would permit the child to occasionally give a drink to the woman next door, but she gave no definite reply except that she thought the woman was sufficiently cared for by her husband. Mrs. Wheeler went there again, and noticed the whip near a chair upon which the little girl was seated sewing, and on this and the previous visit perceived that the child was very shy and nervous and would hardly notice her.

Mr. Howe did not call any witnesses, but proceeded to sum up the evidence, claiming that the jury could not properly convict of a higher offense than assault and battery.

After a brief and forcible address by Mr. Rollins, who argued that the accused should be convicted of an assault, with intent to do bodily harm, the Recorder gave the jury clear instructions upon the law and the verdicts which they might render according to the view they might take of the testimony. The jury retired, and, after a brief consultation, rendered a verdict of "guilty of assault and battery". His Honor, in passing sentence, said he had not the slightest doubt but that the prisoner was guilty of brutal treatment to the child;

Filed *23* day of *April* 187*4*

Pleads,

THE PEOPLE

vs.

Mary Connolly

Felonious Assault and intent to kill

B. K. PHELPS,

District Attorney.

A True Bill.

Benj. H. Day

Foreman.

153

that if the jury had rendered a verdict of a higher grade of assault, he would have imposed the full penalty of the law, as much for an example to others as punishment for her brutal conduct. He sentenced her to the penitentiary for one year.

New York Times, December 27, 1875

LITTLE MARY ELLEN FINALLY DISPOSED OF

In the matter of the child Mary Ellen Wilson, rescued from Mary Connolly, and whose grandparents were alleged to be residing in London, Judge Lawrence yesterday decided that the relatives not having been found, the child should be sent to "The Sheltering Arms". It was the case of little Mary Ellen which led to the formation of the Society for the Prevention of Cruelty to Children.

9

Family Letters and Affidavits

AUTHOR NOTE: Some of the letters are written without proper punctuation and others are written in an unusual, but very contemporaneous style. We have chosen to present them as written, rather than to edit the text in any way. While some of the sentence structure may be unfamiliar and is clearly dated, the style used better reflects the style of speech in the 19th century.

The following pages contain letters written by Mary Ellen's family in an attempt to gain her custody, and sworn affidavits taken by Judge Abraham Lawrence during his efforts to determine where to place Mary Ellen. Within the affidavits are family letters discussing Fanny Wilson and Mary Ellen. Many of these letters were obtained from the archives of the NYSPCC and the ASPCA.

The final letter in this sequence was written to Florence Brasser, Mary Ellen's youngest daughter, in response to a letter written to the NYSPCC by her.

LETTER, MAY 15, 1874, MICHAEL CONNOR (London, England) to (?) E.T. Gerry

> 56 Marsham Street
> Westminster
> London, England

Friday, May 15th, 1874
Sir:

I hope you will please excuse the liberty I take in writing to you. I have also written to Mr. Henry Bergh in case one letter should get mislaid the other might succeed. Sir I received a letter on last Wednesday from New York enclosing 2 small pieces of newspaper containing particulars of inhuman treatment of a child named Mary Ellen Wilson. The letter sent to me had no name or address of the person who sent it so I am quite unable to answer it. Sir it contained your address and the address of Mr. Henry Bergh who with you so kindly interested himself with my poor little grandchild. I was not aware till Wednesday that I had a grandchild living in America. The child's mother was or is if living my eldest child Frances Connor. She went to America in 1858 with her Uncle John Connor since dead. The last time I received a letter from her was in August 1863 she then wrote me from St. Nicholas Hotel. She stated in her letter she was married, that her name was Wilson, and that her husband had enlisted in the 69th New York Irish Brigade. She also said she was leaving her employment because she expected the birth of a child. She said when the war was over she and her husband would come to England to pay us a visit but not to stay for good. Sir I have often wrote since to St. Nicholas Hotel, but I have never heard from her since. I heard from a nephew of mine and others living in New York that her husband was killed in the war. That her child had died and they had no tidings of Fanny, therefore I don't know really if she is dead or living. Sir I wish you would be so kind as to answer this and give me any information concerning how I can get possession of the child Mary Ellen Wilson. Sir my circumstances won't permit me to go to New York to claim my grandchild, of course if the mother is dead I have the nearest claim to her. I see I was described to be worth property. I wish it was the truth for her sake. I now live off of a gentleman named Mr. Bouse, Tothill St. Westminster. Sir I have been out of work turned 6 years. What I had saved by mine and my wife's industry we have been living on. I wish I had known some few years since I had a grandchild living in America I should have been out there. I have another daughter Ellen here in London. She was only 10 years of age when her sister went to America. Sir she says please if it is possible to send her poor long suffering little niece home to where she will receive the love and care which her mother ought but did not give her.

I remain Sir

    Your Obedient Servant
    (signed) Michael Connor

AFFIDAVIT OF ANN ELIZABETH CONNOR, JUNE 2, 1874

Before Hon. Abraham R. Lawrence
A Justice of the Supreme Court

```
-------------------------------------------x
```
In the matter of the custody   )
)
               of   )
)
A child called Mary Ellen   )
```
-------------------------------------------x
```
City and County of New York ss:

Ann Elizabeth Connor being duly sworn deposes and says. She is the wife of Timothy Connor and resides at No. 206 Concord Street, in the city of Brooklyn. That her husband is a working man employed at the present time in the Gas works in the City of Brooklyn in Hudson Avenue. That she and her husband have no children. That her own occupation is that of washer-woman. That her husband is the brother of Michael Connor of No. 56 Marsham Street, Westminster, London, England. That on June 1st deponent's husband received the following letter from his said brother.

Direct your letter 56 Marsham Street
Westminster, London, England

Tuesday May 19, 1874

My Dear Brother,
I received your welcome letter yesterday and was glad to hear you are enjoying good health as Thank God this leaves me at present. I received by the same post a letter from Johnny and one

from Tom McCarthy each letter telling me of poor little Mary Ellen my poor lost Fanny's child, but dear Tim I had heard of her before your letter arrived. I heard first last Wednesday I received a letter dated from New York but whoever sent it gave no name or address they sent me the address of Mr. Bergh and Mr. Gerry the two gentlemen who were the first to take up the poor child's case. I therefore sent two letters on last Wednesday to them therefore they will receive an answer before you. I will also answer Johnny's and Tom McCarthy letters now as the three of you will receive a letter about the same time. I will send you their address – Johnny's address is 401 East 11 Street, New York City. Tom McCarthy's address is No. 1465 2nd Avenue, New York. Tim, I'm sorry to say that things are not going on very brightly just now it is 6 years since I left the Houses [illegible] trial that I was said them with the house I live in off of one Mr. Bower. I am afraid that poor Fanny is dead. I have not heard from her since 1863. Johnny tells me in his letter that she died of hemorrhage of the lungs after 3 weeks illness. He found out her 2nd husband's mother she lives about 4 miles out of the City. Her 2nd husband's name was Gibbon he was a bad head to her he listed in the army. I expect it is but too true about her death but still I can't help feeling doubtful. I fancy if she thought she was dying she would write home to us. I can't make out about her leaving her child so long. Go to Johnny take the letter with you and let him take his letter and go to where the child and show the letters if you like to the authorities there, of course Mr. Gerry and Mr. Bergh will receive their letters first but perhaps you will hear further information of poor Fanny and the child. Of course I expect they will let me have her. You might also call on Tom McCarthy and let him go with you as I have also written to him. Mary is doing a little at the Foreign Office she breaks very fast too what she was she longs to see her Fanny's child. Poor little darling she must have suffered, with that wicked wretch of a woman. I wish to God I had known a few years ago she was living. I should have gone to New York and she would have been spared some years of suffering. Ellen says you are a fine Godfather never mentioned her in your letter but she sends her love to you and her dear little niece Mary Ellen. She is married and has got a fine little Mike. Mother says he reminds her of poor Willie he will be 1 year old on Sunday he sends his love and kisses to his cousin and hopes soon to have her here to share with him his mother's love. Dear brother write back as soon as possible and let me know any further news. Mary joins with me in love to you and the child.

I remain your ever living brother,

Michael Connor

Deponent further says that she is 42 years of age and her husband about fifty, and that they have been married about eleven years. That she became acquainted with her husband's niece Fanny Wilson about that time, and frequently saw her at the St. Nicholas Hotel and she called on deponent frequently. That said Fanny was employed in the laundry at said Hotel.

That shortly after 1865, said Fanny called on deponent at her residence and wanted to borrow some money, and stated that her child was at board with some woman whose name deponent does not remember, and that she, Fanny, was going to live out if she could get some more clothes. That subsequent to that date deponent never saw said Fanny, but has seen the child Mary Ellen now at Police Headquarters, and that said child strongly resembles said Fanny in features and ways.

Sworn to before me this   )
2nd day of June 1874   )
Ann Elizabeth Connor   )

Adolf Leingle (?)
Notary Public
N.Y.C.

AFFIDAVIT OF JOHN CONNOR, JUNE 8, 1874

Before Hon. Abraham R. Lawrence
A Justice of the Supreme Court

```
-------------------------------------------x
```
In the matter of the custody)
)
             of   )
)
A child called Mary Ellen)
```
-------------------------------------------x
```
City and County of New York ss:

John Connor being duly sworn deposes and says that he resides at No. 401 East 11th Street in the City of New York. I am a married man years old and have no children. My uncle Michael Connor resides at 56 Marsham Street, Westminster, London, England. Deponent further says, I knew my cousin Fanny Wilson before and at the time of her marriage. She was about five feet one inch high, dark hair and eyes, broad and somewhat projecting forehead, round face with fair complexion with a little color. She was somewhat stout, weighing about 145 pounds. She was married to Thomas Wilson about 1862. He was an oyster opener in the St. Nicholas Hotel and she was a laundress there. I saw Thomas Wilson once. He was an Irishman about 5 feet 7 or 8 inches high with [illegible], no side whiskers. I believe he went to the war and first enlisted in the 69th Regiment and then reenlisted in the Hawkins Second Fire Zouaves. I met Fanny in Spring Street about this time with a child in her arms which was about three weeks old. She called it by name Mary Ellen and said she had named it after her mother, Mary Connor, and her sister Ellen Connor who is now Ellen Fitzgerald. The child had whitish hair. I stood talking to my cousin Fanny about half an hour. This was about 1863. About two years after this, the next time that I met Fanny Wilson, she said she had put out the child to nurse with a woman, who said the child had died. I did not again see Fanny until 1871, when I met her on First Ave. near Twelfth Street. She then told me that her husband, Thomas Wilson, had died in the war, and that she had married a man named Gibbon, who had also enlisted, and was then on Governors Island. She appeared to be then under the influence of liquor. I met her once after that on First Ave. near Tenth Street. She then said she was living at 525 East Twelfth Street and that she was going to live out. I went there and frequently to inquire after her and after some difficulty ascertained that she died at the Hospital on Wards Island, September 2, 1872 of hemorrhage of the lungs. She must have been then about 34 years old. I learned that her remains had been sent to Bellevue Hospital in the expectation that her relatives would claim them but this was not done and she was buried in the Potters Field. I have been written to more than once by my uncle Michael Connor and also by my cousin Ellen requesting me to make inquiries about Fanny Wilson, which I did, without success. The last letter I so received and which I have was February 2, 1872. I wrote back them all that I ascertained by accidentally meeting her. About May last, reading in the newspapers of this case and I cut them out and enclosed them to Michael Connor. I called at the Police Headquarters shortly since and aw the child Mary Ellen. She bears a strong personal likeness to my cousin Fanny in her face and expression, the chief difference being the color of the hair. About the First of June I received a letter of which the following is a copy, the handwriting of which letter is that of my cousin.

Ellen Fitzgerald
56 Marsham Street, Westminster, London,
England

My dear nephew: May 19, 1874

I thought you had forgotten us till I received your welcome letter yesterday about poor little Mary Ellen. I received by the same post at the same time a letter from your Uncle Tim and another from Tom McCarthy but I had heard previous to that I received a letter last Wednesday direct from New York but the person who wrote it sent their name or address they sent me 2 pieces of newspaper concerning the child and the address of Mr. Gerry and Mr. Bergh the gentlemen who first took the child's case in hand. I therefore wrote off to them the next day as they will receive the letters before you get this. Johnny I always thought Fanny's child had died until last Wednesday. I can't make out who wrote the letter and if no stranger why not give their name and address so as I could answer them. They seemed to take a great interest in Fanny and her child. Johnny I expect it is only too true about poor Fanny's death, but yet I should think she would write to her mother when she was ill. I wish you would ask Mrs. Gibbon the next time you see her for the certificate of Fanny's death, I should like very much if possible, at all, if the child comes to us for you to try and get the certificate, of her mother's marriage with Wilson for the child's sake, if it can be got it would be much better. Whether Fanny is living or dead, I think she aught to have better looked after her poor child not to take a woman's word as to the death of her child but to see to her self or why not have write home to her mother and the child would have been well cared for. May God forgive her. Your Uncle Tim told me in his letter he did not know where you was living but that he had heard where the child is staying that you had been to see the child. I therefore sent him your address also Tom McCarthy. Your uncle's address is 206 Concord Street, Brooklyn. Dear Johnny I thought if you were to go to the place where Mary Ellen is and produce this letter they would give you any information respecting the child so then you could write and let me know if they will let me have the child. Give mine and your aunt's love to your wife and accept the same yourself from your loving Aunt and Uncle.

Michael and Mary Connor

Dear Johnny:

This comes with my love to you and your wife, and family and I am glad you are quite well. I wish to God I had known previous to my marriage that my sister's child was living. I had a great idea of going to America but I did not like to part from my dear mother and father and leave them all alone. I have got a fine boy he is called after Father. He will be 1 year old on next Sunday. Let me know in your next letter if you have any children. Johnny, Fanny's likeness is much faded, after 16 years but I shall get one copied from it and forward it to you. My poor little Darling I do so long to see her, the authorities have never telegraphed or sent us a letter respecting the child – of course Johnny they must let us have the child and if God spares me to her and my boy one would be as dear to me as the other if it should happen to be in spite of 50 husbands.

    I remain, truly yours,
                    Ellen Fitzgerald

Johnny: Give my love and kisses to that poor little Dear and tell her that her Aunt Ellen hopes and prays soon to see her to take her to love as her own little daughter and make up for the sister she knew so little of.

Deponent further says that the following is a copy of a letter received by him from his Uncle Michael Connor and which is in the handwriting of his cousin Ellen Fitzgerald:

February 13, 1873
56 Marsham Street,
Westminster

My Dear Nephew:

I take the opportunity of answering your welcome letter hoping it will find you and your wife and family in good health ass it leaves us at present Thank God for his mercies to us all. Dear Johnny, the last letter I received from you was dated January 1864 it was about your poor Father's death God rest his soul. I have not heard from you since we had a letter from Fanny dated August 1863 and we have not received a line from her since. We have wrote letter after letter both to you and Fanny but have never received an answer. We always wrote to St. Nicholas Hotel, Broadway, for Fanny she never gave us any other directions to write to her. We used to send you letters to Mrs. Murphy until Bill Nagle came home, and he gave us your address at 48 Allen Street, New York City. We wrote the next day to you and we have wrote ever so many letters there since but never got any answer to them so that if you or Fanny wrote to us the letters never came. We left Laundry Yard 3 years ago, but we live at the back in Marsham Street, Smiths old house. I still rent the cottages in Laundry Yard so if any letters went there they would be as safe as ever. Dear John it gives us great pleasure to hear from you to know really that you and Fanny was still living for we did not know what to think. We found out where your Uncle Tim worked from

Bill Nagle and we wrote to him he answered us directly and we had I think 2 letters from him. We always answered his letters but have not [illegible] for a long time. Dear Johnny let us know if you know of how she is situated, and if she has any family. Dear Johnny your grandmother is dead about 18 months she came to see us up to the last and her constant cry was if we heard from you; her son, your uncle John died a few months before her. He met with an accident on the scaffolding at Marlborough House he was taken to the hospital and died there. Give mine and your aunt's love to your wife and family and accept the same yourself from

Your loving Aunt and Uncle,
Michael and Mary Connor

Dear Johnny:

This comes with my love to you and your wife and family and I hope you are all quite well. You asked if I was as fat as ever. Well Dear Johnny I don't think I ever weight more than 10 stone 3 pounds that was before I was married but I don't think I have lost much since – married life seems to agree with me so far. Bill Nagle said you had got much stouter I was glad to hear it for I think it was a great improvement to you. I was married last May at Horseferry Bod Chapel the old place I hope you remember it. My husband sends his best respects to you and your wife and family and hopes he will have the pleasure of seeing you soon. Mother and Father and myself look forward with pleasure at hopes of seeing you Dear

Johnny. Give my love to my dear sister and tell her for God's sake to write to us. Dear Johnny I wish you would send us her direction let me know if she has any family and her husband's name and let me know how many in family you have. Dear Johnny I must now conclude.

I remain your affectionate cousin, Ellen Fitzgerald.

Direct your letters to Mr. Michael Connor Marsham Street, Westminster. My address is Mrs. Fitzgerald, 2 Ponsonby Street, Pimlico. P.S. Kiss your wife and little ones for me. God bless you all and tell her I should very much like to see her and them.

And further deponent saith not
Sworn to before me this
(signed) John Connor
8th day of June 1874.

Adolph Heingle
Notary Public
N.Y. City, N.Y.

**The New York Society For The Prevention of
Cruelty To Children
2 East 105th Street
New York, New York
Cable Address: "GERRY, NEW YORK"
Telephone: Lehigh 4 – 4455**

IN REPLYING, PLEASE REFER TO CASE NO. **1**

Mrs. R. Brasser
Chili, N.Y.

Dear Mrs. Brasser--

It is indeed a pleasure to reply to your letter of the 22nd instant.

You realize, I presume, that the epic story of "Mary Ellen", is known throughout the civilized world, and it was the inspiration of the Movement for the legal protection of children, not only in this country, but throughout the Universe at large.

The story, as given to the general public, is outlined in the 60th Annual Report of the New York Society for the Prevention of Cruelty to Children, a copy of which I am sending you under separate cover.

The details which have not been given out heretofore and which, in the very nature of things, lack much desired data and corroboration, developed in the hearing and proceedings before the Supreme Court, after the rescue of "Mary Ellen" in April, 1874.

So far as this Society can learn from the ancient records, the mother of Mary Ellen was Frances (Fanny) Connor, eldest daughter of Michael and Mary Connor lf London, England. She came to American with an uncle named John Connor in 1858, and in April, 1862 married a soldier in the 69th Regiment named Thomas Wilson, who died during the Civil War. Mrs. Wilson wrote to her father in August63, that she was expecting a child and was leaving her employment, and the child was born during the winter of 1863 or 1864, but the date is not recorded at the Department of Health in this City. The mother left Mary Ellen in the care of a woman named Score and paid for her support.

On July 7th 1865, Mrs. Score asked the Superintendent of the Poor to care for the child, making the following affidavit, viz "Mary Ellen Wilson, aged 18 months, left in charge of deponent until about three weeks since, does not know where the mother lives." On January 2nd, 1866, Mary Ellen was indentured to the woman later known as Connelly and from whose custody she was removed on April 9th, 1874. It developed that her grandfather in London was not in a position to care for her, neither were her relatives then living in Brooklyn and so, for a brief period, she was placed in the Sheltering Arms, and I think it was in June, 1875 that Mrs. Wheeler took her from there to Mrs. D.W. Spencer.

The further circumstances you know and it has been a profound satisfaction to this Society to follow her later career and to know that now, in the evening of her life, she has the comfort of daughters, of whom she is proud.

With every good wish, I am,
Sincerely yours,
 (signed) J.F. Smithers
John F. Smithers,
Manager

10

Bergh's Petition and Judge Lawrence's Response

N. Y. SUPREME COURT
Before Hon. Abraham R. Lawrence

IN THE MATTER OF THE)
CUSTODY OF A CHILD   )
CALLED MARY ELLEN   )

New York, April 8, 1874

The petition of Henry Bergh respectfully shows that a little girl, age about 7 years and called Mary Ellen, is held in illegal confinement and custody by a man and woman named Connolly, at and within the premises No. 315 West Forty-first Street, in the City of New York; that said child is not the child of said man and said woman or either of them, nor are they its lawful guardians or entitled to its custody; that such child is now kept in rigid confinement within said premises by the said man and woman, and is unlawfully and illegally restrained of its liberty, and is sad, has been by them daily, and frequently during each day, severely whipped, beaten, struck, and bruised, without any provocation or cause therefore; and that the marks of said beatings and bruises will appear plainly visible upon the body and limbs of the child at the present time upon inspection thereof; that such child has been kept without shoes or stockings during the entire winter; and that the said man and woman have been for a long time past in the constant and usual habit of leaving the child alone locked up in said premises and allowed to remain there crying for a long time, without any other person whatever therein.

Deponent further states that he has received information from those who reside immediately adjacent to said premises, and in the house in which the child is confined, and whom deponent is ready to produce as witnesses to substantiate the statement by him herein above made, that the said man and woman have repeatedly stated that they had a good fortune for keeping the child, and keep her they would, whatever trouble might be made about it, and that such child was not the child of either of them.

Deponent further saith that the said man and woman have resided only recently in the premises in question, and that he is informed and is able to show by the persons aforesaid, and deponent verily believes, that the said man and woman will carry out of the State, or inflict upon the child aforesaid, or that such child will suffer some irreparable injury, and be further cruelly beaten, and, perhaps maimed, by the said man and woman, before such child can be relieved by the issuing of a Habeas corpus or certiorari.

Your petitioner, therefore, prays that a warrant may be immediately issued, pursuant to the statute in such case made and provided, and directed to such sheriff, constable, or other person as it may be deemed proper, and commanding such officer or person to take such child and forthwith to bring her before you to be dealt with according to law. And further, to arrest and bring before you the said man and woman having such child in his, her, or their custody, to be dealt with according to law, pursuant to the statute in such case made and provided.

And your Petitioner will ever pray.
Dated, New York, April 8th, 1874
                              (Signed) Henry Bergh

City and County of New York ss:
Henry Bergh, the above named petitioner, being duly sworn, says: That the foregoing petition is true to his own knowledge, except to the matters which are therein stated on information and belief, and as to those matters he believes it to be true.

Sworn to before me this}
     (Signed) Henry Bergh
9th day of April 1874

Abraham R. Lawrence
J.S.C

N. Y. SUPREME COURT
Before Hon. Abraham R. Lawrence

IN THE MATTER OF THE   )
CUSTODY OF A CHILD   )
CALLED MARY ELLEN   )

New York, April 9, 1874

Examination had before me Abraham R. Lawrence, Justice of the Supreme Court of the State of New York upon the return of a warrant heretofore issued by me bearing date April 8th 1874, into the facts of the case and into the cause of the confinement or restraint of the child called Mary Ellen named in such warrant, no person appearing to claim or claiming any right to the custody of or control over such child.

The examination begun before me this 9th day of April 1874 and Elbridge T. Gerry appearing as counsel and Ambrose Monell as attorney for the petitioner Henry Bergh Esq. at whose instance such warrant was issued and after Etta C. Wheeler had been by me duly sworn as a witness herein, I did order the matter to stand adjourned until Friday April 10th, 1874 at 10 'clock in the forenoon, and in the meantime and pending such examination did commit the said child Mary Ellen into the custody of George W. Matsell Esq. Superintendent of the Municipal Police of the city of New York, subject to my further order and direction.

11

Testimony of Mary Connolly

NEW YORK SUPREME COURT
      In the matter of the   )
      Custody of a child   )
      called Mary Ellen   )

Hon. A. R. Lawrence
Justice of the Supreme Court
New York, April 10, 1874

Mary Connolly, a witness produced being by me duly sworn testified as follows:

<u>By Mr. Gerry.</u>

Q.   What is your name?
A.   My name is Mrs. Mary Connolly at the present time.
Q.   How old are you?
A.   About thirty-eight years.
Q.   Are you married or single?
A.   I am a married woman at present.
Q.   What is the name of your husband?
A.   Francis Connolly.
Q.   When were you married?

A.   I was married some years ago, about five or six years.

Q.   Have you any children?

A.   I haven't got any living now.

Q.   Did you ever have any children?

A.   I did have children.

Q.   How many?

A.   I had three.

Q.   What were they, boys or girls?

A.   There was two girls and one boy.

Q.   Where are they now?

A.   They are in Heaven, I hope, where we will all be.

Q.   I am not so certain about that.

A.   Well, we expect to. We must not judge. There is another Judge, higher.

Q.   When did your children die?

A.   Well, it is a good many years, eighteen or nineteen. I can not tell really the date.

Q.   Have you been married more than once?

A.   Yes, sir.

Q.   When were you first married?

A.   I was married in 1851.

Q.   To whom?

A.   To Thomas McCormick.

Q.   When did he die?

A.   He died the 15th -I am not really confident of the date, but in August, 1866, with asthmatic cholera. I am sorry.

Q.   Then the children that you have spoken of were his children, were they not?

A.   Yes, sir.

Q.   And they are all of them dead?

A.   The three of them was dead before him.

Q.   They died before he did?

A.   Yes, sir.

The original handwritten court transcripts from the trial of Mary Connolly.

Q.   So that you have no children now living?
A.   So that I have none living.
Q.   What is the occupation of your present husband?
A.   He is a laborer.
Q.   Where do you live?
A.   I live in 315 West 41st Street; it is well known.
Q.   What part of the house?
A.   The upper part of the house.
Q.   How many stories up?
A.   I guess it is three stories. It is a four story building I believe.
Q.   How many rooms do you occupy there?
A.   I occupy two.
Q.   What are they?
A.   What are they?
Q.   Yes
A.   They are dwelling rooms, of course. What do you suppose they would be? Two rooms.
Q.   I am examining you now, and I don't want any argument about it.

179

A.   What should two rooms be?

Q.   What is your particular occupation?

A.   My particular occupation is housekeeping.

Q.   Anything else?

A.   Well, I sleep with the boss.

Q.   Anything else?

A.   Nothing else. I don't mind anything else.

Q.   You don't work for your living in any manner, do you?

A.   I do housekeeping so as to mend and make clean for my husband.

Q.   And that is all?

A.   I keep his house clean and himself clean too.

Q.   That is all you do?

A.   I do that, and that is a great deal for a woman to do; if she does it in a proper manner it is a great deal for a housekeeper, if she does her own work. Not everybody does it.

Q.   Do you know this child in court, this Mary Ellen?

A.   Certainly, I should know her.

Q.   She has been in your possession for sometime, hasn't she?

A.   Since the 2nd day of January, 1866.

Q.   Where did you get her from?

A.   I got her from Mr. Kellogg.

Q.   Who is he?

A.   Don't you know the gentleman?

Q.   I ask you the question, who is he. I don't want any question put to me. Answer the question.

A.   Mr. Kellogg; don't you know him? I don't know who he is if he ain't some of the Commissioners.

Q.   Where did Mr. Kellogg reside when you got that child?

A.   Down town. What makes me forget where he kept his office? He removed to 11th Street; I disremember.

Q.   What is his first name?

A.   George Kellogg, I have it on the paper.

Q.   Did you know him before you went to see him about the child?

A.   Well, I hadn't known him ever in my life until I went to him about her.

Q.   Did you apply for this particular child?

A.   I did; I applied for her.

Q.   How did you come to apply for this particular child?

A.   I wanted to keep her as my own, of course.

Q.   Did you know anything about the child previously to applying to Mr. Kellogg?

A.   Well, I did know that she was there. I had knowledge that the child was there, left as an orphan.

Q.   Whom did you learn from?

A.   I learned that from my husband-my first husband.

Q.   Was the child any relative of your first husband?

A.   Sometimes he says she was, and more times he says she was not, and I felt bad for the child when I heard him say that, and I would say "Well I will take her out."

Q.   What relative did your first husband say she was of his?

A.   I understood that she was his.

Q.   His child?

A.   Yes, sir.

Q.   Did your first husband ever tell you who the mother was?

A.   No, he would not tell me. I have often wanted him to. He said she was around, but that she was good for nothing, that she was a good for nothing thing; it was not worth making mention of her, and she is living yet.

Q. Do you know who she is?

A. No, I wish I did. I would have given her to her long, long ago. I am sorry I hadn't left her with Mr. Kellogg and let him find her out, for of course he knows where she is.

Q. When did your first husband first tell you about this child?

A. He told me in 1855.

Q. What did he say then as near as you can remember about it?

A. He says, "I have a young one over in the Home and as we have nary one, I wish you would see after it and get it out."

Q. How long after you were married was that?

A. It was a good long time; I cannot tell how many years. I never counted it or reckoned it up.

Q. He told you in 1855 you say?

A. Yes, sir.

Q. And what year were you married in to him?

A. 1851.

Q. And he told you this in 1855?

A. Yes, sir.

Q. When were you married the second time?

A. I was married in about six years and I guess again next August, or six years last August I think or September.

Q. Six years last August?

A. Yes, sir, about the latter end of August or the commencement of September I was married six years.

Q. About 1867 then?

A. Yes, sir, something about that.

Q.   When did you say you got the child?

A.   I got her the 2nd day of January, 1866.

Q.   When did your first husband die?

A.   He died in August, 1866.

Q.   So that you got the child before your husband died, then; you got it in his lifetime, did you?

A.   No, I did not get it in his lifetime.

Q.   You got it before your husband died, didn't you?

A.   I got it before my husband died. I guess there was more than her to be had; there is two more; there is three of them

Q.   Where?

A.   They must be there.

Q.   How do you know that?

A.   Well, he told me he had three.

Q.   Did he give you their names?

A.   He did not. I wanted to know if he had got a boy there. He said, "It makes no difference to you." So this time he got out that one.

Q.   Did he get this child out and give it to you?

A.   He helped to get it out. He signed his hand to it. I have his paper here today; he signed his hand to it, and Mr. Kellogg signed it.

Q.   Where are the papers; have you got them with you?

A.   Yes, sir, I have got them.

Q.   Let me have them will you. I will give them back to you.

A.   I thought I could see Mr. Kellogg myself this morning but it was rather late to wait for him. Yes, he has got three; there is two more there.

The witness produced the paper referred to, which is marked "For identification, April 10, 1874, F.M.A." and of which the following is a copy:

"This indenture witnesseth: that Mary Ellen Wilson aged one year and six months hath put herself and by these presents and with the consent and approbation of the Commissioners of Public Charities and Correction of the City of New York doth voluntarily and of her own free will and accord put herself to adopt to Thomas McCormick, butcher, and Mary his wife, residing at 866 Third Avenue in the City of New York, and after the manner of an adopted child to serve from the day of the date hereof for and during the full end and term of sixteen years and six months next ensuing. During all of which time the "said child her parent faithfully shall serve, his secrets keep, his lawful commands everywhere readily obey; she shall do no damage to her said parents nor see it done by others without preventing the same so far as she lawfully may, and give notice thereof to her said parent; she shall not waste her said master's goods nor lend unlawfully to any; she shall not absent herself day nor night from her said parent's service without his leave nor frequent ale houses, taverns, nor play houses and in all things behave herself as a faithful child ought to do during the said term; and the said parent shall use the utmost of his endeavor to teach or cause to be taught or instructed the said child in the trade- and mystery of housekeeping and plain sewing, and procure and provide for her sufficient meat, drink, apparel, mending, lodging and washing fitting for an adopted child and cause her to be instructed in reading, writing and arithmetic during the said term; and at the expiration thereof shall give a new Bible to the said child and a suit of new clothing in addition to her old ones in wear, and shall furnish to her at all times when necessary or proper, medical assistance and attendance and nursing, and at all proper times the utensils and articles required for keeping her healthy and cleanly.

Special. To report to the said Commissioners of Public Charities and Correction once in each year the character and condition of said girl. And for the due performance of all and singular the covenants and agreements aforesaid the said parties bind themselves unto each other firmly by these presents.

In witness whereof the said parties have interchangeably set their hands and seal hereunto. Dated the Thirteenth day of February in the nintyeth year of the Independence of the United States of America and in the year of our Lord 1866.

Signed and delivered
Thomas McCormick (Seal)
in the presence of Mary McCormick (Seal)
H.W. Boswell
George Kellogg   (Seal) Superintendent O.D.P.
for Mary Ellen Wilson."

On the back of the paper is the following endorsement.

New York, Feb. 15, 1866. "City of New York) ss.

We consent to and approve of the within indenture providing all the requirements are complied with.

On behalf of the Board of Commissioners of Public Charities and Correction.

Attest. James Bowen   Isaac Bell
        Secretary.   President.

This indenture is not transferable nor can it be cancelled without the consent of the Board of Commissioners of Public Charities and Correction."

Q.   It was your first husband, Thomas McCormick's suggestion then that you should take this child, if I understand you right?

A.   Yes, sir.

Q.   And you agreed to do it?

A.   I agreed to do it.

Q.   And you knew at the time it was his illegitimate child, did you?

A.   Well, he told me so.

Q.   You hadn't any doubt about it then had you?

A.   I hadn't quite knowledge of it. I always believed what he said, be it right or wrong in regard to such a thing as that. I thought the man was in earnest for I had heard tell of him before that and I didn't mind if he had ten of them.

Q.   How come you to select this one child, Mary Ellen Wilson, out of the three that were there; did you select it or he?

A.   I selected it, I took her, but I didn't know which the others were.

Q.   Were they all named Wilson?

A.   Well, her name was Wilson and she put her in under her name.

Q.   Do you know who the mother was or her husband? Do you know her first name?

A.   No, I know her name is Wilson, by getting it in that way.

Q.   That is the only way?

A. That is the only way.

Q. Do you know whether the child is named after her mother at all?

A. Well, Mr. Kellogg of course has it on the books. He says it is her and that she put her in there and that he called her after her own name.

Q. Were you present when Mr. McCormick your first husband applied to Mr. Kellogg for this child?

A. He went along with me.

Q. You were there with him?

A. Yes, sir.

Q. What did your husband state to Mr. Kellogg at the time?

A. He stated that there was a child there and he would like to get it out.

Q. Did he tell Mr. Kellogg that the child was his?

A. No, sir, he did not.

Q. What did he say to Mr. Kellogg about it?

A. He did not want to let on anything about it, and he let me go and do all that was necessary.

Q. What did you do?

A. I told him there was a child there and I would like to get it and he says, "Well, does any neighbors know who you are, or are you able to give support to the child?" and I said yes, and I knew the family doctor.

Q. Who was your family doctor then?

A. The family doctor was Mr. McLaughlin who lived on Sixth Avenue.

Q. Where does he live now?

A. I didn't see him not since my husband died. He used to attend my husband.

Q. Do you recollect his first name?

A. I don't recollect his first name. Dr. McLaughlin I used to see on the paper.

Q .An old man or a young man ?

A.   He was not an old man; he was about as young as you, six years ago.

Q.   You have no idea where he resides now?

A.   No, sir.

Q.   Where did he live on Sixth Avenue?

A.   He was near Twenty-eighth Street.

Q.   Do you recollect which side of the way it was?

A.   The West side.

Q.   Above or below Twenty-eighth Street?

A.   It was near the Eighth Avenue.

Q.   Sixth Avenue, I thought you said?

A.   It was between Sixth -no, it is in Sixth Avenue I think, near Sixth Avenue.

Q.   Just think one moment.

A.   It was near the Eighth Avenue. I was there once for medicine for him and I don't very well recollect the number. It was in Twenty-eighth Street, I think, near Eighth Avenue.

Q.   Was it on the upper or lower side?

A.   It was nearer to the Eighth Avenue.

Q.   On which side of the street, upper or lower?

A.   Down town, I guess.

Q.   The down town side?

A.   On the down town side, and you go over to the Eighth Avenue.

Q.   On the left hand side as you go towards Eighth Avenue?

A.   Yes, sir, at that time, it would be easy to know where he lived.

Q.   Did Mr. Kellogg put any inquiries to you as to your connection with the child in any way, as to the child being a relative of yours?

A.   No, sir, I didn't let on to him anything about it.

Q.   Did you tell Mr. Kellogg why you wanted the child?

A.   I told him I wanted that child out, that I should like to keep it for myself. I had an idea from my husband of course telling me that there was three there of his, and that he would like to have one out; and I said I would like to have a little girl. There was two girls and a boy.

Q.   You don't know the name of the others do you?

A.   No, I do not.

Q.   Were they all named Wilson?

A.   I suppose she named them when she put them in.

Q.   Were they all named Wilson?

A.   They must be named that when they were there. If she named one she must have named them all. Likely she might.

Q.   Did your husband ever give you any possible clue as to where this woman called Wilson lived?

A.   No, sir, he never told me where she lived, I often asked him.

Q.   Did he say whether she was in New York or not?

A.   Sometimes he said she was out of New York and more times he would say she was in the city.

Q.   Was the child delivered to you immediately on your signing this paper? This is your signature, isn't it?

A.   Yes, sir.

Q.   And your husband signed the paper here, didn't he, at the same time?

A.   At the same time.

Q.   And then Mr. Kellogg signed this paper?

A.   We had the child from the 2nd of January, but we signed that paper and it was not ready for us when we got the child out, and I went on the 15th; the date is there on the l5th.

189

Q.   So that you had the child on the 2nd of January and the paper was not executed until the l5th?

A.   Until the l5th.

Q.   Did you have any paper given to you with the child when you took it on the 2nd of January?

A.   No, sir.

Q.   This child was given to you without any paper whatever being signed by you?

A.   That is so.

Q.   No receipt given for the child?

A.   No receipt nor nothing.

Q.   And you never signed any paper. I want to be accurate about this.

A.   Yes, you are welcome.

Q.   Neither you nor Mr. McCormick signed any paper then?

A.   No paper but this.

Q.   This is the only one you signed?

A.   That is the only one. They thought that was enough I suppose.

Q.   About how old is this child?

A.   Well, I have her since 1866, the 2nd day of January, 1866 up to the present period, I suppose it is over seven years, may be past seven years, isn't it?

Q.   What I want to get at is this; is this statement in the paper which you have that the child was aged one year and six months when you took her in 1866- is that correct as near as you believe?

A.   I believe it must be nearly correct. Of course Mr. Kellogg gave in the statement that he got himself.

Q.   Then the statement was not made by your husband as to the age of the child? That is what I want to get at.

A.   It was made by the mother when the child was taken in.

Q. Do you know whether this child has now any relatives in the world?

A. Well, I don't know if that woman didn't die since.

Q. You say you don't know her?

A. I don't know her, and she may be living. I understand from many people that the mother is living, and father some place; they can tell about as many fathers as they have a mind to.

Q. Whom did you hear anything about where the mother of the child was living, from?

A. My husband told me sometimes that she lived down town, and he would not tell me the street or number, and I often wanted to see her since I have got the child.

Q. That you have stated, you told me a moment ago that you had learned from several persons about the mother of the child. Now I want to know who those persons are.

A. Friends of my own that were acquainted with my husband; many friends would say, "Don't you be foolish."

Q. Who are they?

A. I cannot give the names, boys or young men or people when they get drinking together, and they would say, "Well, don't be foolish, you know McCormick has got a lot of children; don't be foolish, don't give up your sense for it." I said, "I don't care if he has ten or twenty; let him fire away."

Q. Where were they drinking?

A. In his own house.

Q. Were you drinking?

A. Yes, I took a glass of lager.

Q. Anything else?

A. No, sir.

Q.	What were they drinking?

A.	They were drinking lager too.

Q.	Who were the other young men?

A.	I cannot say; he used to be working along with them and used to come along with them from the market, and allover.

Q.	Can't you tell a single word that they told you about the mother of this child.

A.	When they came they said, "Don't fool with McCormick; he has enough of them."

Q.	Who were they?

A.	I can't tell, I don't know their names. I had no harm or else I would find out, of course. I didn't make no harm of it; it was only for play and joke's sake as people do joke and play that way in drinking and in company. They can say many pleasant words and I don't mind what they say.

Q.	Have you ever seen any of those persons since?

A.	No, sir.

Q.	Have you ever seen any person since your husband's death whose name you now remember who ever told you anything about this woman, the mother of this child?

A.	No, I wish I did know where she was.

Q.	Have you any means of ascertaining who the mother of this child is?

A.	No, I have not if Mr. Kellogg don't tell me, or tell you.

Q.	I am not speaking of Mr. Kellogg now.

A.	He is the only one that will give you information, and find her out.

Q.	Do you know of any relative of this child?

A.	No, sir.

Q.	Did you ever hear that she had any relative excepting what you have mentioned?

Q. Have you ever received anything from any person for the support of this child?

A. Not one cent.

Q. Have you ever been promised anything by anybody for it?

A. Never one cent, although they have me scandaled in the papers for it. I am thankful to the gentlemen for their scandal about me.

Q. Has anyone called on you in relation to this child or spoken to you about the child?

A. No, sir, not in relation to the child.

Q. You took possession of this child on the 2nd day of January?

A. Yes, sir.

Q. Were you then living at 866 Third Avenue?

A. Yes, sir.

Q. And was your husband, Thomas McCormick, then a butcher?

A. Yes, sir.

Q. Did the child live with you?

A. Yes, sir.

Q. Did you take it as an apprentice or as an adopted child?

A. I took it as an adopted child; I could not get it out in any other way, as long as the mother left it in there and she was living, and he said she was useless and it had better be taken out in that way for fear she might call for it. If she would mind it of course she would take it back again.

Q. Did you ever teach or cause to be taught, or instruct this child in the trade and mystery of housekeeping and plain sewing?

A. Well I understand as I read there that when she grows up of course I will do it, and I would do it. I teached her the alphabet and she can say it for you.

Q.   Is that all you have taught her?

A.   I teached her the Lord's prayer.

Q.   Did you ever tell her that there was a God?

A.   I did, I believe in God myself.

Q.   I am not asking you about your own individual belief.

A.   When you ask me about God I believe that there is a God; I understand that God created me.

Q.   You do?

A.   Yes, and all humans; I understand it. I thank him for His mercy to us. I understand that there is a Lord God.

Q.   Did you ever instruct that child that there is a God?

A.   Yes, sir.

Q.   Did you ever teach that child to pray?

A.   I teached her the Lord's Prayer.

Q.   Did you ever teach her what would become of her if she told a lie?

A.   I did often, and she is first rate for it.

Q.   Just answer my questions. Did you ever teach her the solemnity of an oath?

A.   I believe I did not.

Q.   Did you ever teach her what would become of her hereafter if she told a lie?

A.   I told her she would go to the bad place if she told lies. I often teached her that.

Q.   Did you ever teach her what you meant by the bad place?

A.   Yes, that God wouldn't give her any place in Heaven.

Q.   Did you so explain it to her?

A.   I did, indeed.

Q.   During the time that that child was with you did you ever instruct her - I want you to answer me the question - did you actually teach her the trade and mystery of housekeeping and plain sewing?

A. Well, I couldn't, for the child is too young to learn housekeeping yet; she hasn't become a housekeeper yet.

Q. That is your idea, is it?

A. Well, a child of eight or nine years old she wants her book, more than she wants to do housekeeping I understand.

Q. What books did you ever teach her?

A. I teached her the alphabet as far as to say small spelling and such as that. You can try her.

Q. What books did you ever teach her to spell from?

A. Nothing but a plain spelling book.

Q. What plain spelling book?

A. Child's reading book, I have paid five and ten and fifteen cents for books for her such as that, and the Primer.

Q. What clothing did that child have when she came with you?

A. She just had about as much as she has now.

Q. Nothing else?

A. Nothing else. What was on her was plain and simple, plain clothing. (Officer Evans produces the wardrobe of the child.)

Q. Is this plain clothing; just look at it and see whether that is the plain simple attire which you say she had when she came to you?

A. That is about the same. She has had a petticoat such as that, not as good as that, when I got her at the place.

Q. She had a petticoat when she came out of the Asylum, did she?

195

A.   Yes, sir, she has a clean one now. I am not ashamed of what I wash. I am but a very humble woman myself, I can't be a lady; I can't play lady no how.

Q.   You say when she came to you she had a flannel petticoat?

A.   Yes, sir.

Q.   What became of it?

A.   The flannel petticoat?

Q.   Yes.

A.   I let her wear it out.

Q.   Did you ever replace it?

A.   Indeed I did. What would keep a child six or seven years? Have you been the father of a child and know what clothes you want for six years? I think you are man enough for that.

Q.   I am examining you.

A.   You charge me with it and I ask you what would a child wear out in six years? I am the master over the child and I keep her clean too. You are not to do that.

Q.   Has that child now a plain petticoat?

A.   Yes sir, it is very plain and clean.

Q.   Has the child any other clothing in your possession excepting what is now produced in court?

A.   No, she hasn't got any more clothing.

Q.   Was the child ever sick during the time she was with you?

A.   She never was sickly.

Q.   Never was?

A.   She never was sickly, a healthy kept child, I always kept her comfortable; she always got enough to eat and had a good warm fire, better than myself.

Q.   This paper contains the following clause. At the head of the paper it says -Please take notice of the Special clause to this indenture. "Go report to the said Commissioners of Public Charities and Correction once in each year the character and condition of said girl." Did you ever make any such report?

A.   Yes, sir.

Q.   How many times did you ever report to the Commissioners of Public Charities and Correction after you got this paper the character and condition of the child?

A.   I took her down there twice and that is all.

Q.   Only twice?

A.   Only twice.

Q.   When was the first time you took her down?

A.   I don't know exactly; I didn't put down the date of the year; I didn't heed when I brought her down.

Q.   How long after you first got her?

A.   I had her then nearly a year. I brought her down there and he was very proud of it indeed.

Q.   When was the next time you brought her down?

A.   In the next year; the month I couldn't recollect.

Q.   Since that time you have not brought her down?

A.   No, I didn't bring her down since because I saw they paid no attention to her. They were satisfied I didn't need to bring her any more there.

Q.   Who paid no attention to her?

A.   The gentleman said she seemed to be well enough off.

Q.   Did they tell you that you need not come again?

A.   They did not tell me that I need not come again.

Q.   You can read can you?

A.   I can read.

Q.   And you have read this paper through haven't you?

A.   I read it a couple of times.

Q.   Did you at any time learn from anyone connected with Mr. Kellogg or his office there that they knew who the mother of the child was?

A.   Well, I understand that when the name is taken in the office that it will be there and they ought to know who she is.

Q.   Did they ever tell you?

A.   They told me of course that her mother left her there and that she went by the name of Wilson.

Q.   Did they ever tell you anything more about it?

A.   Nothing more about it. Of course he knows all about it.

Q.   But you don't know?

A.   I don't know anything about it more than that. He told me that she was put there and that was the name of the mother. She gave her name.

Q.   What is the full name of your present husband?

A.   Francis Connolly.

Sworn to before me this)
Mrs. Mary Connolly
 l3th day of April 1874)
Abm. R. Lawrence
JSC

12

Testimony of Alonzo S. Evans

NEW YORK SUPREME COURT
In the matter of the   )
Custody of a child   )
called Mary Ellen   )

Before Hon. A.R. Lawrence
Justice of the Supreme Court
New York, April 10, 1874

<u>Alonzo S. Evans. a witness produced being by me
duly sworn testified as follows:-</u>

<u>By Mr. Gerry.</u>

Q.   What is your present business?
A.   Officer of the American Society for the Prevention of
      Cruelty to Animals.

Q. At the request of Mr. Henry Bergh you made some inquiries about this child did you not, in the house, before the application was made to the judge for the warrant?

A. Yes, sir.

Q. Did you accompany the officer who brought the child down and executed the warrant?

A. I did, sir.

Q. I want you to state what if any thing took place between yourself and the person who has last been on the stand, Mrs. Mary Connolly, on the occasion of your first going there, what you saw if anything of the child and what occurred

A. The day before the arrest I went there and got the name of the family and procured the name of the child. That is all I did the first day.

Q. Did you see the child on that occasion?

A. Yes, sir.

Q. Did you make any inquiries of the woman in regard to its being her child or not?

A. I did, sir.

Q. What did she say?

A. She said it was not her child.

Q. Did she say anything else?

A. No sir, she was very close mouthed.

Q. Did you see the child on that occasion?

A. I did, sir.

Q. How was the child dressed?

A. The same as she is now.

Q. What did the child do when you went into the room?

A. She ran into the corner of the room and crouched down in the corner and held her arms up as if she thought I was going to strike her.

Q. Did you make any gesture?

A. Not at all.

Q.   What did the woman do?

A.   She looked at me and inquired my business, and I told her.

Q.   Gave her the information?

A.   I did sir.

Q.   When did you next see her?

A.   I saw her the next morning about nine o'clock, or between eight and nine, I think.

Q.   Where did you see her then?

A.   I saw her in her own room.

Q.   In these premises in 4lst St.?

A.   Yes, sir.

Q.   Was the child with her?

A.   Yes, sir.

Q.   State, if you please, what occurred in the room?

A.   I went in with an officer.

Q.   What officer?

A.   Officer McDougal.

Q.   Officer McDougal of the Central Office?

A.   Yes, sir.

Q.   State now all that took place in detail.

A.   I went in and the officer told her who he was – made his business known.

Q.   Did he show the warrant?

A.   He did, sir.

Q.   What did she say when the warrant was shown to her?

A.   She said, do what we liked with the child, only she wanted to know what we were taking the child for.

Q.   Did she make any other remark to you?

A.   No, she was talking one thing and another. She went to the other end of the room and sat down and commenced to laugh.

Q.   To laugh?

A.   Yes, sir, a kind of a peculiar smile I don't know whether you could call it a smile; she did not laugh out loud.

Q.   Where was the child when you entered the room?

A.   It was, I think, standing half way across the room as if she heard the knock and was expecting to see somebody come in, and I looked to see who it was coming in the door.

Q.   Did the child go near her?

A.   No sir, the child ran away from her and ran into the bedroom.

Q.   Did the woman address any remarks to you while you were there?

A.   Not on that visit she did not. On the second visit she did.

Q.   Then you and the officer took the child?

A.   We took the child.

Q.   Where did you take the child to?

A.   Took her to a close carriage outside.

Q.   When the officer took the child to put it in the carriage outside what clothes did she have on?

A.   It had nothing on at all but what it has got now.

Q.   Did you ask for anything else?

A.   I went immediately back to the room and asked for a cloak or something to put around the child. She said the child had nothing and she would not give me anything at all.

Q.   What then did you do?

A.   I stopped and got a lap robe and wrapped around the child.

Q.   Where was the child taken to?

A.   To Police Headquarters. Superintendent Matsell's office.

Q.   What then was done?

A.   She was then brought from there down here.

Q.   No. I am speaking about you. I want you to state all that occurred, what passed between yourself and this woman on that occasion, either at the time of the arrest or at the time the child was taken, or shortly after?

A.   Then we went back the second time.

Q.   Who went back with you?

A.   Officer McDougal and Officer Dusenbury.

Q.   State what occurred the second time when you went back. About what time in the morning was the child taken?

A.   I think it was about half past nine or quarter past nine.

Q.   Then you drove down to Police Headquarters?

A.   Yes sir.

Q.   And then you went back again?

A.   Yes sir.

Q.   For what purpose did you go back the second time?

A.   For the purpose of getting the wardrobe that belonged to the child.

Q.   State what occurred the second time when you went back. Was the woman there, Mary Connelly?

A.   Yes, sir.

Q.   You went into the room?

A.   Yes sir

Q.   What transpired?

A.   I asked for the wardrobe belonging to the child. She said the child had nothing at all. I asked for what she did have and took those two garments that you have shown here this morning. In the meantime the child had said she had been struck with a pair of scissors.

Q.   Where did the child state that?

A.   In the Superintendent's office.

Q.   Who was present then?

A.	I guess half a dozen; the two officers were present and Superintendent Matsell and several others standing around.

Q.	Did the child show you where she had been struck?

A.	I asked her what the mark was on her face and she said it was done with a pair of scissors, that her mother was ripping some work and she held it and she did not do it right, and she struck her.

Q.	Have you got the scissors?

A.	Yes, Sir.

Q.	Where are they?

(Witness produced a pair of scissors)

Q.	This is the pair of scissors that the child said she was struck with?

A.	Yes sir, she identified them at the Superintendent's office.

Q.	You took these to the Superintendent's office?

A.	And she identified them and attempted to take them out of my hand, as if I was going to give them to her and she was going to take possession of them. She knew the scissors the minute she saw them.

Q.	What occurred on this second visit of yours to the premises where this Mrs. Connolly was?

A.	We went there for the wardrobe and searched for a certain cow-hide which was supposed to be there - which was known to be there in fact.

Q.	Did you find that?

A.	We could not find it, sir.

Q.	What next transpired? What did she say to you, if anything on that second occasion?

A.	She was very impertinent and passed some remarks to me.

204

Q.   Obscene remarks?

A.   One remark I considered was very obscene, it is not fit for the ears of the court. I prefer not to say what it was.

Q.   You can mention it in private to the stenographer who will take it down?

A.   She asked me if I would not like to come up and see her quietly, and asked me where I lived.

Q.   What then did you do?

A.   We found that we could not find any more wardrobe belonging to the child, or anything more, and we then left and went immediately back to Police Headquarters, and were directed by the Superintendent to bring the child.

Q.   Did you have any further or subsequent conversation with this woman Mary Connolly at any time?

A.   She said to me that the clerk of Mr. Kellogg told her quietly that he knew who the child belonged to, but that she would not tell us.

Q.   Did she give the names of that clerk?

A.   She did not, no sir.

Q.   Was anything else said that you now remember by this woman?

A.   Well, there were several remarks passed that I did not think of any consequence at the time.

Q.   While you were in that room did you have an opportunity of examining the condition of the apartment at all?

A.   I looked around the room.

Q.   How many beds were there in the room?

A.   There was only one room.

Q.   How large a bed is there in it?

A.   What we would call a three quarters bed.

Q.   Did you see any place for this child to sleep in?

A.   No, Sir, except in one corner. The child told me she slept up in one corner of the room under the window.

Q.   Did she show you where she slept?

A.   No, Sir.

Q.   Did she state what she slept on?

A.   No, Sir.

Q.   Did the child make any statement to you at any time since you have had her in custody, during these last two days since you have been with her, in relation to her having been beaten in any manner?

A.   Yes, Sir, she said she had been struck on the face with a cow-hide, and on the leg with a cow-hide, and she had been struck on the head with a cow-hide.

Q.   What did she say about the matter in regard to who it was struck her?

A.   She said she was struck by this Mrs. Connolly, her mother, she called her.

Q.   When did she first tell you about having been struck by Mrs. Connolly?

A.   The moment I got her in the carriage.

Q.   What did she say the moment you got into the carriage?

A.   She was very timid. Officer McDougal took her on his lap, and I went to speak to her and she cringed as if she expected a blow, as if she expected I was going to strike her, and I asked her where she was whipped and how many times, and she stated.

Q.   What did she say?

A.   She said she was whipped every morning.

Q.   By whom?

A.   By this Mrs. Connolly.

Q.   With what?

A.   With a rawhide.

Q.   Where?

A.   On different parts of the body. She showed the marks where she had been struck.

Q.   What marks did she show you?

A.   She showed marks on her head, and marks on her face and on her leg.

Q.   A rawhide whip?

A.   Yes, Sir.

Q.   Is there anything further that you can mention in connection with this matter?

A.   Nothing more that I can think of just at present.

Sworn to before me this 13th day of April 1874
Alonzo S. Evans

Abm. R. Lawrence

13

Testimony of Christian B. McDougal

NEW YORK SUPREME COURT
In the matter of the   )
Custody of a child   )
called Mary Ellen   )

Before Hon. A. R. Lawrence
Justice of the Supreme Court

New York, April 10, 1874

<u>Christian B. McDougal</u> a witness produced being duly
sworn testified as follows:

    <u>By Mr. Monell</u>

Q.   What is your occupation?
A.   A member of the Police Force of the City of New
    York.
Q.   Did you see Mrs. Connolly on the stand this
    morning?
A.   Yes, Sir.

Q. Have you ever seen her before?

A. Yes, Sir.

Q. When?

A. Yesterday.

Q. Under what circumstances?

A. I received a warrant issued by Judge Lawrence of the Supreme Court for the production of a child, and I went in company with the witness who was on the stand last.

Q. Mr. Evans?

A. Yes, Sir, with the understanding that he would direct where to find her and I accompanied him.

Q. Where did you go to?

A. It was 41st St. near Eighth Avenue. I did not notice the number. It was something that had to be attended to very quickly and I did not notice.

Q. Did you go into Mrs. Connolly's room?

A. I did.

Q. How many rooms did she have?

A. Two.

Q. What did you do when you got to Mrs. Connolly's room?

A. I seized the child immediately upon its being pointed out by the witness who was on the stand last.

Q. And did what with it?

A. After a little hesitation I took her out of the building to the carriage.

Q. Then you did not go back the second time?

A. No, Sir I wrapped my coat around the child to cover her nakedness and took her to the coach.

Q. And took the child down to Police Head Quarters?

A. Yes, Sir.

Q. Did you go back the second time?

A. Yes, Sir.

Q. What took place then?

A.   In company with the witness who was on the stand last, Mr. Evans, and Mr. Dusenbury we made a reasonable search for this cowhide that the child said she had been struck with, and to demand the wardrobe of the child. This was upon the direction of the Superintendent.

Q.   You were unable to find the cowhide?

A.   We found nothing.

Q.   What did you say to Mrs. Connolly about the wardrobe?

A.   I said to her, "We want the clothing belonging to this child, all of it."

Q.   What did she reply?

A.   She produced them after a little hesitation.

Q.   This clothing that has been produced here in court?

A.   Yes, Sir.

Q.   Is that all?

A.   I said to her "Is this all?', She replied "Yes." "Every article?" "Yes." "How long," I said, "has she been with you". "Six years." Six years?" I replied. "Yes Sir." "And this is all the clothing the child has?" "Yes, that is all."

Q.   Did you ask her for shoes or stockings?

A.   I asked for all her clothing.

Q.   What was the condition of the child as regards clothing, when you took her away?

A.   As you see her, excepting the blanket which was procured by Mr. Evans on the way down.

Q.   No shoes or stockings?

A.   Nothing but as you see her.

Q.   What was the condition of her body in regard to bruises or marks of any kind?

A.   When I got in the coach with her I retained her on my lap and covered her up with my coat and I said to her, "What is that mark upon the side of your head? She replied that her mama done it. "Did your

Mamma strike you?" "Yes Sir". "What did she strike you with?" She replied, "A pair of scissors." "A pair of scissors? Did she strike you with a pair of scissors?" She replied in the affirmative. I said "What did she strike you for?" She replied, because she did not hold the cloth right, something that she was holding while her mamma, as she said, was cutting it. The mark is on the left side of her head.

Q. Did she speak about any other bruises?

A. I asked her what the other bruise on the side of her head was. She said that was from a cowhide which her mother struck her with.

Q. Did she say anything about her being whipped by her mamma?

A. Yes, Sir, she said in general terms that her mother had whipped her repeatedly, and was in the habit of whipping her.

Q. Did she say what she used to be whipped with?

A. No Sir, nothing more than the cowhide.

Q. With a cow-hide?

A. Yes, Sir, with a cow-hide.

Q. When you went back the second time to Mrs. Connolly's house what was Mrs. Connolly's action, what did she say and what did she do; how did she deport herself when you went back to get the child's wardrobe?

A. She appeared to be very much excited and used language accordingly.

Q. Did she make use of any obscene remarks?

A. She made use of a very impudent remark I thought.

Q. If it is not proper to state it here will you state it in answer to my question to the reporter. State anything she said of that character.

A. She told this Evans, "You are a pretty man," or "you are a nice looking man. Would you like to come and see me?" That was about it.

Q. Did you ask Mrs. Connolly anything about the parentage of this child?

A. No, Sir.

Q. Did you ask her whether it was hers?

A. No Sir, but she complained of the abrupt action. I told her I had to be a judge of that because I said I came here for a duty and I said I must be the judge of how I should perform it, so long as I did not abuse anyone. She replied then, "Well why didn't you say so; why didn't you tell me?" I said "I did tell you," I said I had my shield on, which I did. She didn't make any objections to the child being taken, particularly.

Sworn to before me this 13th day of April 1874
C. B. Macdougal

Abm. R. Lawrence
JSC

14

Testimony of Thomas Dusenbury, Charlotte Fiehling and Catherine Kemp

NEW YORK SUPREME COURT
In the matter of the)
Custody of a child)
called Mary Ellen)

Before Hon. A. R. Lawrence
Justice of the Supreme Court

New York, April 10, 1874

<u>Thomas Dusenbury,</u> a witness produced being by me duly sworn testified as follows:

By Mr. Monell

Q.   What is your occupation?
A.   Police Officer.
Q.   Of the Municipal Police?
A.   Yes, sir.

Q.   Attached to the Central Office?

A.   Yes, sir.

Q.   Have you ever seen this Mrs. Connolly who has been on the stand this morning?

A.   I saw her yesterday.

Q.   Yesterday for the first time?

A.   Yes, sir.

Q.   Under what circumstances; how did you happen to see her?

A.   About the same circumstances that Officer McDougal has just stated.

Q.   You went there for the purpose of executing the warrant?

A.   Yes, sir.

Q.   Did you go there twice?

A.   No, sir.

Q.   You were only present on the second visit?

A.   Yes, sir.

Q.   Won't you state as near as you recollect what took place, the occasion of your going the second time, and what took place when you got there?

A.   We went to get the wardrobe of the little girl. We asked the lady for it, Mrs. Connolly, and she handed us out those two pieces. We asked her if that was all she had.

Q.   The clothing that has been produced here in court?

A.   Yes, sir.

Q.   You asked her if that was all?

A.   Yes, sir.

Q.   What did she reply?

A.   She said that was all the little child had. I asked her if she hadn't any shoes and stockings and she said she had not.

Q.   What was Mrs. Connolly's deportment at the time of your visit?

A.   Very abusive I should think.

Q.   Did she make use of any abusive remarks at all?

A.   Yes, sir.

Q.   Please state them to the reporter, what she said of that nature.

A.   She asked this Mr. Evans how he would like to come back and stay with her, "Would you like to come and stay with me?"

Q.   Did she say anything in your hearing in regard to having whipped the child?

A.   Yes, sir, I asked her what she was in the habit of whipping her with, whether it was a raw-hide or scissors or poker. She said she had often whipped her with her hand.

Q.   Did she say anything about if she got her back what she would do with her?

A.   She said she would whip her again and whip her as often as she chose.

Q.   Did you see the child when it was brought to Head Quarters the first time?

A.   No, sir, I did not.

Sworn to before me this 13th day of April 1874
Thomas Dusenbury

Abm. R. Lawrence
JSC

Case #1: The Mary Ellen Wilson Files

NEW YORK SUPREME COURT
In the matter of the   )
Custody of a child   )
called Mary Ellen   )

Before Hon. A. R. Lawrence
Justice of the Supreme Court

New York, April 10, 1874

Charlotte Fiehling, a witness produced being by me duly sworn testified as follows:

By Mr. Gerry

Q.   Where do you live?
A.   325 West 41st Street.
Q.   How long have you lived there?
A.   I suppose a year, in Mrs. Bingham's house.
Q.   Do you know Mary Connolly who has been on the stand this morning?
A.   I know her, I have seen her once or twice when I lived there.
Q.   You lived there in the same house with her. Where did you live with her, in what house?
A.   West 41st Street, Mrs. Bingham's house.
Q.   What number?
A.   325.
Q.   Do you know when she left there?
A.   Yes, sir.
Q.   When did she leave there?
A.   I don't know how long she is away from there.
Q.   Two or three years ago?
A.   No.
Q.   Three or four months ago?

A. Yes, sir, three or four months ago.

Q. How long did you and she live together in this house of Mrs. Bingham's?

A. A year.

Q. So that you lived in the house with her a year before she moved to the house where she now is, where she has been about four months?

A. Yes, sir.

Q. Have you ever seen this little child Mary Ellen before?

A. Yes, sir, I have only seen her twice since I lived there.

Q. I want you to state as fully as you can what you have seen about the child and what you have seen Mary Connolly do to the child.

A. I cannot say that I saw her do anything to her, although one day she went out down in the yard and she went to the watercloset, and her mother was not at home, and she had nothing on but a little bit of a petticoat and no shoes and no stockings. It was very cold and I took hold of her little arms and said, "My little child why don't you put shoes and stockings on?" and she said she daresn't, and I said "Why," and she said "My mother will not let me," and she was all black and blue.

Q. You saw the marks, did you?

A. I saw the marks, and I wanted to take her up stairs with me, and she would not go, she said she daresn't.

Q. Did you ever hear that child cry while you were there?

A. Yes, sir, I heard her cry different times.

Q. How near was your room to this room of Mrs. Connolly's?

A. I lived on the top floor and I passed there going out and in.

Q. You passed the room that Mrs. Connolly was in?

A. Yes, sir.

Q. And you heard the child cry?

A. Yes, sir, often.

Q. Did she cry very loud?

A. Yes, sir.

Q. What else did you hear if anything?

A. I can not say.

Q. Did you ever have any conversation with Mary Connolly about the child?

A. Yes, sir, I was once sitting in the yard one evening and I told about whipping the child black and blue and I said if that goes to law she would have been punished for it, and she said anybody what interferes with that she would go through the highest law with them.

Q. Is that all that you can state about the matter?

A. That is all.

Sworn to before me this 13th day of April 1874
Charlotte Fiehling
Her (x) Mark

Abm. R. Lawrence
JSC

NEW YORK SUPREME COURT
In the matter of the)
Custody of a child)
called Mary Ellen)

Before Hon. A. R. Lawrence
Justice of the Supreme Court

New York, April 10, 1874

<u>Catherine Kemp,</u> a witness produced being by me duly
sworn testified as follows:

<u>By Mr. Gerry</u>

Q.   Where do you now reside?
A.   325 West 41st St.
Q.   Did you reside at any time in the same house with
      this woman who has been on the stand, Mary
      Connolly?
A.   Yes, sir.
Q.   Where was it?
A.   On the same floor at 325 West 41st St.
Q.   That is the house which was kept by Mrs. Bingham?
A.   Yes, sir.
Q.   And where she was four months ago before she
      moved to her present house?
A.   Yes, sir.
Q.   How long did you reside in that house kept by Mrs.
      Bingham?
A.   I lived there two years and ten months I believe.
Q.   Have you ever seen this little child Mary Ellen?
A.   Yes, sir.

Q.   I want you to state all you know or have seen or heard in regard to that little child and Mrs. Connolly's treatment of her?

A.   All I saw the child was locked all day except when the child was going in the yard once in a while going to the water- closet. That is all what I saw the child. And it was very seldom too. I did not see or hear any licking. That is all I can say.

Q.   She was locked in the room?

A.   In the room all day.

Q.   Did you ever see this woman take her out at anytime?

A.   Never.

Q.   Was she ever allowed to go out of the room during these two years that you were there?

A.   No, sir.

Q.   Never was?

A.   No, sir.

Q.   You would have seen it and known it if she had, wouldn't you?

A.   The child went out when her father was home and the mother was gone. That is the way the child slipped out in the hall. I lived on the same floor.

Q.   The same flat with her?

A.   Yes, sir.

Q.   The same floor?

A.   Yes, sir.

Q.   Next door to her?

A.   Next door.

Q.   And the child during the whole of that two years and six months that you were there in that place never was allowed to go out of the room at all but kept locked up?

A.   Except when I saw her around when the father was in the house and the mother was gone; that is all. She could run out and run in again.

Q.   Was she kept in close confinement there?

A.   She was kept in the back room.

Q.   Kept in there all the time?

A.   Yes, sir.

Q.   Did you see the child while she was there?

A.   I saw it about twice or three times in the room, but when I went into the room the child slipped back in the room, so I could not see anything of the child.

Q.   The child ran away from you?

A.   Yes, sir.

Q.   Did you see how the child was dressed on that occasion?

A.   She was barefooted and with a dress on.

Q.   Was the dress the same as she has on now?

A.   The same.

Q.   Nothing on her legs?

A.   I can't say.

Q.   And that lasted for the two years and six months that you say she was there?

A.   Yes, sir. Mrs. Connolly lived there about two years.

Q.   It was during this time that you say she was kept in this close confinement?

A.   Yes, sir.

Q.   Did you ever examine her to see if there were any marks on her at all?

A.   I never examined the child, the child was always scared; she trembled always. As soon as she saw the mother come she was always trembling.

Q.   As soon as she heard Mrs. Connolly come she was always trembling?

A.   Yes, sir.

Q.   Did she retire in any way or draw herself up?

A.   I cannot say.

Q.   When she was locked up in this room who was there – anybody?

A.   No sir, all alone.

Q.   Locked up alone in this room?

A.   Yes, sir, sometimes all day very late.

Q.   Did she have anything to eat during that time?

A.   I cannot say.

Q.   You did not give her anything did you?

A.   No, sir, I did not have a chance.

Q.   You don't know of anyone that went there?

A.   No. sir.

Q.   You knew the door was locked?

A.   The door was locked, and the shutters shut sometimes, and she had blinds and some curtains so that you could not see through.

Q.   That was the common course during the whole of the two years that she was there?

A.   Yes, sir.

Q.   Did you ever hear her cry?

A.   I heard her cry but I made no remarks, I did not hear her licked.

Q.   You heard her cry several times didn't you?

A.   Yes, sir, but I made no remark on that.

Sworn to before me this 13th day of April 1874

Catherine Kemp

Abm. R. Lawrence

JSC

15

Testimony of Mary Studer, Margaret Bingham, Charles Smitt and Jane Slater

NEW YORK SUPREME COURT
In the matter of the   )
Custody of a child   )
called Mary Ellen   )

Before Hon. A. R. Lawrence
Justice of the Supreme Court

New York, April 10, 1874

<u>Mary Studer,</u> a witness produced being by me duly sworn testified as follows:

<u>By Mr. Gerry</u>

Q.   Where do you now reside?
A.   323 West 4lst Street.
Q.   Have you ever lived in the same house with Mary Connolly who was on the stand this morning?

A.   No, I never lived together with her, but I lived in the next house adjoining.

Q.   How long have you lived in the next house adjoining?

A.   Three years and a half.

Q.   Where was this house adjoining, in the front or rear?

A.   They joined in the rear and in front, both ways.

Q.   Have you ever seen this little child Mary Ellen now in Court?

A.   I never saw it before; I saw it for the first time today.

Q.   Do you know anything about the treatment of this child by Mary Connolly, if so state what you know on the subject, or have seen or heard?

A.   I never saw anything; I heard a great deal.

Q.   State all that you heard?

A.   I did not understand what the people who told me about it said, because I don't understand English.

Q.   Did you hear any noise of beating or crying of the child?

A.   Yes, sir, I very often heard the child crying as if it was beat by somebody.

Q.   How often did you hear this?

A.   I cannot tell exactly how many times but it has been a great many times.

Q.   Where were you when you heard the sound you have mentioned?

A.   Every time I was in the rear room. I never heard it in the front room.

Q.   Did you hear the sounds distinctly?

A.   Yes, sir, I heard the child distinctly cry.

Q.   Was this a matter of frequent occurrence?

A.   I very frequently heard the child crying and I very frequently heard sounds as if the child was beat by somebody.

Q.   You heard the sound of blows, then, did you?

A.   I very often heard as if the child was slapped with the hand by somebody and the child commenced to cry.

Q.   Was this a matter of daily occurrence?

A.   I did not hear it every day but very often.

Q.   Have you ever examined this child to see whether she had any bruise on her or not: Have you ever seen any marks on the body?

A.   This is the first time that I have seen the child, today.

Sworn to before me this 13th day of April 1874
Mary Studer

Abm. R. Lawrence
JSC

NEW YORK SUPREME COURT
In the matter of the   )
Custody of a child   )
called Mary Ellen   )

Before Hon. A. R. Lawrence
Justice of the Supreme Court

New York, April 10, 1874

<u>Margaret Bingham,</u> a witness produced being by me duly
sworn testified as follows:

<u>By Mr. Gerry</u>

Q.   Where do you now reside?
A.   325 West Forty-first Street.
Q.   Do you know the witness Mary Connolly who has
      been on the stand this morning?
A.   Yes, sir, I have seen her this last year.
Q.   Did she ever board in the same house with you?
A.   No sir, she lived in the rear house and I lived in the
      front.
Q.   Have you ever seen this child Mary Ellen who is in
      court now?
A.   Yes, sir.
Q.   I want you if you will, to quietly state all that you
      know, have heard or seen, in relation to this woman
      Mary Connolly and this little girl Mary Ellen,
      including any statement that Mary Connolly may
      have made to you at any time. Just tell your story
      right out.
A.   Well, I think it was two years last September that
      she came around one day and wanted some rooms.
      My daughter went to show her the rooms and she
      said she would come back in the evening with her
      husband and that she liked the rooms; and they
      came back in the evening and took the rooms, and I
      said "Have you any children; what family have
      you?" "Well" she says, "I haven't any family." Says
      she "Yes, we have one child but" says she, "my child
      wont give you any trouble or anybody else." Says I,
      "It is not for that, for where the parents live they
      must have their children but", says I, "half grown
      boys are sometimes very troublesome, but I don't

mind little children; we have some of our own."
They took the rooms and moved in and the night
they came it was after dark, and she brought the
child and it had on a little apron such as that, and a
petticoat-that came about here (indicating) and an
old hood. They came in, and I suppose some
months after that my daughter said -

Q.   What is the name of your daughter?

A.   Jane Slater. Jennie says, "They cannot have any
child there, Grandma for I have never seen a child."
This was some months after they moved in. Says I,
"Yes, they have a child for I saw it when they took it
in, and she often told me it was just the age of your
eldest." "Dear me," says she, "how can they keep it
there?" The windows were fastened down tight,
and the blinds were down; and this building has a
kitchen at the back, a bedroom in the middle, and a
sitting room in the front and the child was always
kept in back, and my son here if he had any errand
to go in, as soon as ever he touched the door the
child would run like a hunted deer into the back
room, and we never could see her. So I felt very sad
and many times wept over it, and finally I said if I
knew where to go I would go and make complaint,
but the people told me that the police would not
listen to me, and I didn't know about this Cruelty to
Animals, and I think this is just as great cruelty as
ever there was. This lady was around visiting the
sick, and she had heard about it, and she asked me
if so and so was the case, and I told her yes, and she
asked how I bore it. Well, what could I do? The
lady visits me sometimes and when I saw her last
she enquired if that child was still a prisoner.

Q.   What is the name of that lady?

A.   Mrs. Freeman is her name, a lady and a Christian too, and she said her heart ached when she thought of it. Mrs. Connolly and Mr. Connolly used to quarrel sometimes, this time I guess she got the worst of it. I went across the yard in the morning and I told her I couldn't have it, it made it very unpleasant, that one family could make an annoyance in the whole house, and that I could not have it so, that I wanted quiet sober people or else my place empty.

Q.   What did you hear about the child?

A.   Says she, "It is all his fault he is all the time fighting me to put this child in an asylum or poor-house, and when I got it I got a good fortune with it to take care of it, and I am going to take care of it."

Q.   Whom did she say she got that good fortune from?

A.   I didn't ask her. Says I, "Mrs. Connolly, It seems very hard to keep that little child locked up in the house all the time," and she dare not put her nose out of the window. Well, she wouldn't let her out to learn such language, and says I, "we have four little ones and we try to keep them as nice as we can, and we don't allow them to use bad language, and if you can not let her out you ought to send her to school." The child knows me and if she happened to see me when she had her nose out of the window she would call me and I would ask her if she was hungry, but the child could not get the window up more than that (indicating).

Q.   Not more than an inch?

A.   Not more than an inch. Mrs. Connolly would go away in the morning and seldom came back until after dark, and left that child locked up. That was done repeatedly, it was not once or twice.

Q.   Do you know anything about the beating of the child?

A.   I never have seen her beat.

Q.   Did you hear the child cry at anytime?

A.   I heard her crying but I suppose she always took her into the back room to whip her and then there was a bedroom and the sitting room between the yard and that room. Mrs. Studer heard it more than I did. Mrs. Kemp lived on the same floor with her. Mrs. Studer lived there was a wall between them; but I saw her get enough of bad treatment. She did run up to me one evening, and says I, "Mary dear, how did you get out?', "Well, mother went out, " says she "and she didn't lock the door, and father went for beer and he didn't lock it and then I just run out." Says I, "Are you hungry?" I got her something. Says I, "Run in my dear." When she had a cut across here.

Q.   A cut across the chin?

A.   Yes, sir.

Q.   How large a cut across the chin?

A.   Well, as if it was the point of the scissors or the edge of a knife; it was not a whip.

Q.   Could it have been made by such an instrument as that (producing the scissors)?

A.   Yes, sir, something like that; I couldn't say what it was done with.

Q.   That was sometime ago; that is worn off?

A.   Oh, yes, that is a year ago I suppose.

Q.   Did you ever examine the child at all or see any other marks on her except that cut?

A.   I never had a chance.

Q.   Did you ever go into the room of this woman Mary Connolly while she was there?

A.   Yes, sir.

229

Q.   Did you ever see anything there in the shape of a whip or cow-hide?

A.   I never could see anything. As soon as I knocked at the door the child ran into the back room.

Q.   You never saw a cow hide?

A.   I never did. She didn't keep it there; I don't know where she kept it, she probably kept in the back room where she punished the child.

Q.   How was the child clothed during the whole of that time?

A.   Just about the same as she is now. My daughter used to say if she would only take her out with her when she would go out and let her get the air it would not be so bad, but I never saw her take that child out with her from the day she came to the day she left except on one occasion, she never took her on the street.

Q.   There is nothing else that you can state is there that you can remember?

A.   No, sir.

Q.   What is the name of your son?

A.   He don't know much about it.

Q.   About how long ago was this matter that you have mentioned?

A.   About her running out?

Q.   Yes, during the time that she was with you, about how long was it before she moved to her present house?

A.   Two years and three months she was in our house.

Q.   And she moved from there about four months ago, didn't she?

A.   The 1st of December. She moved in in September and she stayed there and she found people getting in a stew and she left.

Q.   She left about the 1st of December last?

A.   Yes, sir.

Q.   Were you the housekeeper of the house?

A.   I was the owner of it.

Q.   She hired the rooms of you?

A.   Yes, sir.

Q.   Is your daughter here?

A.   Yes, sir.

Q.   I omitted to ask you -you will pardon me; I would like to know how old you are?

A.   Next month I will be sixty-nine.

Sworn to before me this 13th day of April 1874
Margaret Bingham

Abm. R. Lawrence
JSC

NEW YORK SUPREME COURT
In the matter of the   )
Custody of a child   )
called Mary Ellen   )

Before Hon. A. R. Lawrence
Justice of the Supreme Court

New York, April 10, 1874

Charles Smitt, a witness produced being by me duly sworn testified as follows:

By Mr. Gerry

Q.   What is your name, residence and occupation?

A.   Charles Smitt, 315 West Forty-first Street next door to Mrs. Connolly.

Q.   Is it the same house with Mrs. Connolly.

A.   Yes, sir, next door to it, a room and bed-room.

Q.   A room and bed-room adjacent to hers?

A.   Yes, sir.

Q.   What is the name of your wife?

A.   Mary Smitt.

Q.   Is she an invalid at the present time; is she sick?

A.   Yes, sir.

Q.   Very sick?

A.   Yes, sir.

Q.   Hardly expected to live?

A.   No.

Q.   A dying woman?

A.   Yes, sir.

Q.   Do you know and have you ever seen this little child Mary Ellen, before today?

A.   Sometimes I have seen her a little bit when the door was open about that wide (indicating), but just as soon as she saw me coming out of my door she would go and shut her door. She was afraid of everybody. I was in the room twice on New Year's day. That was all I ever saw the girl. I never saw her shoes on her.

Q.   Or stockings?

Q.   No, sir.

Q.   What did you see when you were in the room there. Do you recollect seeing any whip there at all?

A.   The most of the time I am not at home. My woman knows more than I do, but she is not able to come down here.

Q.   I want to know simply what you know about the matter.

A.   I heard a good many times she get a licking.

Q.   You have heard it?
A.   Yes, sir.
Q.   What have you heard?
A.   She always was hollering "Mama" and traveling from the bed room to the front room, and she was going behind and licking her.
Q.   You heard that?
A.   I heard that myself.
Q.   Did you hear the blows?
A.   Yes, sir.
Q.   Did you hear the child cry?
A.   Yes sir, she always was hollering "Mama!"
Q.   And crying with pain?
A.   Yes, sir.
Q.   How often has this occurred, recently?
A.   Most every morning.
Q.   For how long a time back?
A.   Well I didn't hear anything in two weeks yet.
Q.   You have not heard it for two weeks?
A.   No, sir.
Q.   Previous to that time the child was whipped every morning?
A.   Yes" sir.
Q.   To your knowledge?
A.   Pretty near most every morning.
Q.   About what time was this in the morning?
A.   About seven or half past seven and so on or eight o'clock.
Q.   Where was Mr. Connolly about that time?
A.   He was going to work every morning.
Q.   What time did he go to work?
A.   About seven o'clock.
Q.   How long did this whipping last?
A.   About a quarter of an hour or so, as soon as she got tired.

Q.   Did you ever examine this child to see whether she had any marks on her?

A.   No, I didn't see her.

Q.   Never got a chance?

A.   No, sir, if she saw somebody coming from down stairs, or if I opened my door and their door was a little open she came and run and shut the door. I couldn't see her, I got no chance, I never went into the room.

Q.   Did you ever have any conversation with Mrs. Connolly about this child?

A.   No, she only told my woman.

Q.   I want to know what she told you.

A.   Not me. She only told me that her husband was making a hook on the bedroom and if she goes out she locks her in.

Q.   How long has this whipping been going on?

A.   Since they lived there.

Q.   Since last December?

A.   Yes, sir.

Q.   How long have you been in the house?

A.   Three years.

Q.   So that you were there when she came?

A.   Yes, sir.

Q.   How near the rooms which are occupied by this Mrs. Connolly is the bed in which your wife is sick at the present time?

A.   I have got a bed in the front room, I daren't put a bed in the bedroom you know, it is too cold in there.

Q.   How near the room of Mrs. Connolly is it?

A.   Only the hall way.

Q.   Is your wife confined to her bed the entire time?

A.   Yes, sir.

Q.   She is there all the time is she?

A.   If I have to make the bed I have got to lift her out.

Q.   But she is there the entire time sick in bed?

A.   Yes, sir.

Q.   In a dying condition?

A.   Yes, sir.

Q.   You never saw this little child go out of the room?

A.   No, sir.

Q.   What effect did the cries which you have mentioned which you heard of this child have upon your wife; did it produce any effect on her?

A.   Certainly.

Q.   What effect did it have?

A.   She was crying last night for it.

Q.   Did you ever hear her complain to anyone about it?

A.   No.

Q.   She spoke to you about the matter didn't she?

A.   Yes, sir.

Q.   Your wife did?

A.   My wife, yes, sir. She knows more than I do; I don't care much about it.

Q.   You mean you don't know much about it?

A.   Yes, sir.

Sworn to before me this 13th day of April 1874
Charles Smitt

Abm. R. Lawrence
JSC

NEW YORK SUPREME COURT
In the matter of the   )
Custody of a child   )
called Mary Ellen   )

Before Hon. A. R. Lawrence
Justice of the Supreme Court

New York, April 10, 1874

<u>Jane Slater,</u> a witness produced being by me duly sworn
testified as follows:

By Mr. Gerry

Q.   Where do you reside?
A.   325 West Forty-first Street.
Q.   You are a daughter of Mrs. Bingham?
A.   Yes, sir.
Q.   Will you state what you know about this matter in
      connection with this little child Mary Ellen, and
      also the treatment of it by Mary Connolly who has
      been in Court produced today as a witness?
A.   I never saw her strike her or heard any cries or saw
      any marks, but I never saw her outside of the door
      or playing in the yard like other children. When she
      first came there in the summer she would
      sometimes go away three or four days a week and
      stay until night. Her husband did not come home to
      dinner. The shutters were shut always and the
      windows closed and I insisted on it there was no
      child there, because I never saw it, but my mother
      said she was. It was for some months before I saw
      her.
Q.   This was all during the hot summer?
A.   Yes, sir, and a very hot summer it was, two years
      ago.
Q.   It lasted for months?
A.   It lasted all that summer. When she was in the
      house, she never had the shutters or window open.

Sometimes you could see her sitting by the window herself but you would never see the child. I would often try to see through the shutters to see if I could see her but I never yet saw the child. She would sit sometimes sewing but I never saw the child.

Q.   Did you ever see the child out of the room at any time?

A.   Yes, summer before last I think it was one day she was out. It was Saturday and the children were all playing in the yard and the little thing opened the window and shutters and she wanted to come out of the window and none of the children would take her. Mrs. Kemp lived on the floor and of course she didn't want any trouble with Mrs. Connolly and the little thing wanted to come out but she didn't come out, and after a little while she shut the window down and fastened the shutters all tight before Mrs. Connolly came back. When Mrs. Connolly came home she heard that she had had the window open and after that she had catches put on the window so that she couldn't open the window. After that time the shutters were never open when she would go out.

Q.   Did you ever have any conversation with Mrs. Connolly about the matter?

A.   No, sir.

Q.   When you saw the child on this occasion when she came out was she dressed any different from what she is now?

A.   Just about the same. Sometimes she had a little apron on or a little dress.

Q.   No shoes or stockings?

A.   Yes, sir, once the first summer they moved there she was once outside in the yard and was dressed very neatly, with shoes and stockings and a little white dress and she played about half an hour. That is the only time that I ever saw her out to play or saw her dressed. My mother says one Sunday she went out with Mr. Connolly's sister; she went out dressed up with her as if to visit. I didn't see her at that time. The sister of Mr. Connolly was there at that time.

Q. Do you know her name?

A. I don't know her name. I suppose it is Connolly but I don't know her first name. A sister of Mr. Connolly was stopping there.

Q. Is that the person they call Winnie?

A. I don't know.

Q. Is there anything else that you can state?

A. I don't recollect anything else. I never saw her out unless once in a while when she would hang out clothes I would see the little thing peeping around.

Q. Trying to look out?

A. Yes, sir, and I have known her to be there fastened in in the winter and summer; she would be closed up all day. That is all I know. I never have seen bruises or anything like that.

Q. Have you ever heard her cry?

A. No, I have not heard her cry. I never was there near enough the house.

Q. You have children of your own haven't you?

A. Yes, sir.

Q. Did you ever ask this Mrs. Connolly to let her child play with yours?

A. Yes, sir.

Q. She never did let her play with yours?

A. She never would because she said the other children would contaminate her. She didn't want the child to hear the language that the children used.

Q. Whereabouts is this room situated in Mrs. Bingham's house.

A. Where Mrs. Connolly lived?

Q. Yes.

A. On the first floor.

Q. How many rooms did she occupy there?

A. Three.

Q. What did she pay for those rooms?

A. $10.50 a month.

Sworn to before me this 13th day of April 1874)
Mrs. Jane Slater

Abm. R. Lawrence
JSC

16

Testimony of Etta Wheeler, Mary Smitt and Mary Webb

NEW YORK SUPREME COURT
In the matter of the   )
Custody of a child   )
called Mary Ellen   )

Before Hon. A. R. Lawrence
Justice of the Supreme Court

New York, April 10, 1874

<u>Etta A. Wheeler,</u> a witness produced being by me duly sworn testified as follows:

By Mr. Gerry

Q.   You attended, did you not, Mrs. Smith?
A.   I did occasionally.
Q.   Will you state under what circumstances you attended her, and what you there learned in

reference to this matter and what communication you made on the subject to Mr. Bergh about it?

A.   I was told I think about the middle of December by a person named Mary Litzbeney who for sometime has lived in Mrs. Bingham's house that Mrs. Bingham wished her to say to me that there was a child living at 315 West 41st St. who had up to within two weeks before perhaps - I am not positive of the length of time -lived in the rear of Mrs. Bingham's house, a house owned by Mrs. Bingham; that during the two years that the child lived there she had been very cruelly treated. I was told substantially what has been given in evidence today about the confinement and beating etc. Mrs. Bingham through a woman whom I had never seen then, requested me through this third party to do something.

Q.   Did you call on Mrs. Smith?

A.   I went to 315 West 4lst St. I asked them on the first floor if a woman named Connolly was living in the house. I was told there was and I was told the room where she lived -the top floor, on the right hand. I went to the top floor and knocked at the door of the left hand room; I received no reply. I opened the door and saw a very neat orderly room perfectly clean. I went in and looking into the bedroom which was a little at the left I saw a woman lying in bed. I went in and spoke to her, and as I had gone there hoping to get some excuse for going into the other room, as I was assured by the people in 325 that I would not gain admittance to the room being a stranger. I hoped to find some reason in this other room for going to that room. I found a sick woman. I talked with her; I saw that she needed attention and such attention as I could give her. I told her that I would endeavor to befriend her through the winter and I said to her "You have a neighbor; does she come in to see you." She said "Yes, sir, she comes in to see me and seems very kind." The woman at that time was lying upon a bed in the bedroom.

Q. You mean Mrs. Smith?

A. Yes, sir, Mrs. Smith was lying in the bedroom. The bedrooms belonging to the suite of rooms are separated by the stairway and the hall. You can hear nothing from one room to the other. I asked if there was a little girl there. She said she thought there was, she had not seen her. I said then, "I will leave something for you. I will ask that woman to let the little girl come in and wait upon you and if you make friends with the little girl she will be a comfort and help to you this winter as you have no children of your own."

Q. Did you subsequently attempt to see Mrs. Connolly?

A. I left the room then and went to Mrs. Connolly's room. She did not ask me to come in but I went in uninvited and sat down. I then saw for the first time Mrs. Connolly and this little child.

Q. That is now in Court?

A. Yes, sir. The little child was washing dishes from a pan, standing upon a little keg turned before the table. She was taking the dishes up from the table and washing them. She paid no attention to me, no more I think than as though I had not gone into the room, as though she was not conscious of my presence. Across the table lay a whip; it is what I call a rawhide.

Q. It lay across the table?

A. It lay across the table from which the child was taking the dishes. It was about that length, as near as I can tell.

Q. Nearly three feet long?

A. About a yard I should call it. It was leather twisted together, large at one end and small at the other, and painted green. The child acted in a very nervous manner. I did not speak to her; I ignored her presence entirely. I got into conversation with the woman about her sick neighbor and asked her to go in and attend to her a little and offered to send some things to the woman through her, some things that should be uncooked, and broth, if she would heat it for her. As the husband was away at work and the woman entirely alone through the day. I was satisfied in my own mind that the reports that I had heard were true and I went away.

Q. What reply did Mrs. Connolly make to this suggestion of yours -this offer of yours?

A. It was not a frank reply. I judged that she wished me to understand that she would comply, but at the same time I did not think that she meant it. She never spoke to me frankly.

Q. Did you have any further interviews with Mrs. Connolly?

A. I did. I can give no dates.

Q. Will you state anything that transpired at any of those interviews?

A. I went in again. The second time that I went in the child was seated in the farther part of the room and had evidently been sewing; she was sewing while I was there. I sat down for a few minutes uninvited and I talked with Mrs. Connolly. The raw hide at that time was lying across a chair which stood near the stool upon which the child was sitting. The only time I ever spoke to the child, before I saw her yesterday, I said then in an involuntary way while I was still talking with the woman - I turned and said "Come and see me dear , will you?" The child started nervously to her feet and she advanced one step towards me and then dropped again. I paid no attention to the matter whatever and went away. My talk with Mrs. Connolly was always confined to the care of the sick woman. I have been several times purposely upon the coldest, bleakest days we had through the winter to see Mrs. Smith, fearing that she might be alone, as she often was, and hoping at the same time that I might find the child more comfortably clothed, but she was always dressed as she is today with the exception of the first time. She then had on what I judge to be the little apron that was shown here this morning.

Q. How was this room of Mrs. Connolly's heated?

A. There is a stove, a common cooking stove.

Q. Is there any stove in the bedroom at all?

A. I have never seen the bed room. I have looked into the bedroom. No there can be no stove in it.

Q. Did you see the child at any time outside of Mrs. Connolly's room?

A. Never. I have often in going up the stairs seen the door a little ajar perhaps that distance (Indicating). The child always appeared to me to be on the guard and shut the door immediately. I have always every time, except the first that I went to see Mrs. Smith, in going into the house looked to the windows of Mrs. Connolly's room and have never once seen the curtains raised.

Q. How large a room is this room which is occupied by the Connollys?

A.   I cannot say. If I should give a guess which is very unreliable, it may be 16 ft. square.

Sworn to before me this 13th day of April 1874)
Etta A. Wheeler

Abm. R. Lawrence
JSC

NEW YORK SUPREME COURT
In the matter of the   )
Custody of a child   )
called Mary Ellen   )

Before Hon. A. R. Lawrence
Justice of the Supreme Court

New York, April 10, 1874

Deposition of Mary Smith a witness in behalf of the petitioner in the above proceeding, taken in pursuance of the annexed order.

The said Mary Smith being duly sworn testifies and says:

By Mr. Stetson

Q.   What is your name?
A.   Mary Smith.
Q.   How old are you?
A.   Pretty near forty five.
Q.   Have you been sick long?
A.   Yes, sir for eight months. I am in the bed three months steady.

Q.   Are you very sick?
A.   For three months I am very sick. Eight doctors have given me up.
Q.   Does the doctor come to you any more?
A.   Oh, yes sir.
Q.   Do you hope to get well?
A.   No, sir. I am satisfied I shall die.
Q.   You expect to die?
A.   Yes, sir.
Q.   And what you say now is said as a dying woman would say it?
A.   Yes, sir.
Q.   How long have you lived here?
A.   Three years.
Q.   Who lives in the room next on the right?
A.   Mrs. Connolly.
Q.   How long has she lived there?
A.   I guess about four months.
Q.   Have you ever seen a little child called Mary Ellen here?
A.   I saw her twice; I did not speak to her.
Q.   What have you ever heard about that little child?
A.   I have heard her when I have lain here. I cannot say more than that I heard her. She (Mrs. Connolly) licks her all the time every day most in the morning before she gets breakfast.
Q.   About what time in the morning?
A.   I don't know exactly. The man goes to work; he has got eight hours work. Sometimes she got licked before he went away and sometimes when he was gone. If she did not get licked in the morning she would through the day. She would get it sometimes twice in the day.
Q.   Always every day?

A. Always every day. She has not got any in three or four days.

Q. When was the last time you heard it.

A. I cannot say that, I have not got much in my head.

Q. Do you think you heard it last Sunday?

A. No not Sunday; she didn't get any Sunday.

Q. Did you hear it at any time last week?

A. Yes, sir, I am sure she got it during the last week.

Q. Has Mary Connolly ever said any thing to you about it?

A. No, sir.

Q. Never a word.

A. Never, she daresn't come out the door.

Q. Who?

A. Mary Ellen; she daresn't come out the door.

Q. How do you know that?

A. She was afraid. She would see somebody and go and hide. I have seen her twice. She had the broom in her hand and she saw me and went back in the door, and locked the door.

Q. Did you hear screaming?

A. I heard her scream. Mrs. Connolly licked her and the child ran from the corner down in the bedroom and she ran back, up and down, up and down, and she hollered "Oh, Mamma! Oh, Mamma!" and I heard her strike her with a cow-hide, and she ran up and down hollering, "Oh, Mamma!"

Q. Could you hear the blows?

A. Yes, sir. I could hear everything.

Q. Did you ever know of the man whipping her?

A. I never heard the man lick her, never. I never heard a bad word from the man.

Q. Always from the woman?

A.   Always from the woman. It makes me so sick sometimes I am so heart sick when I hear that little child.

Q.   Did you ever see this cow-hide?

A.   I saw it once; the first week when she moved in I saw the cow-hide.

Q.   How was it that you happened to see it?

A.   It was lying on the table, I believe.

Q.   Her room is just the other side of that partition at your left hand?

A.   Yes, Sir.

Q.   Whenever you go out your door her door opens right in the other side of the partition?

A.   Yes, sir.

Q.   And when you go out your door you can look into her room if the door is open?

A.   Yes sir, and she can look in here.

Q.   And as you were going out your door when they first came in you saw this cow-hide in their room?

A.   Yes, sir the first week when she moved in.

Q.   Is it a large cow-hide?

A.   I don't know that. It was lying on the table. It is about the kind that a man uses when he rides on horseback, about that size (indicating) about two feet and a half long, I guess.

Q.   As large around as your finger?

A.   It has got something on the end as large as your finger; I don't know how many.

Q.   It has got ends to it?

A.   Yes, sir.

Q.   You mean lashes?

A.   Yes, sir.

Q.   Like a cat-o-nine-tails?

A.   Yes, sir, I don't know how many is on it.

Q. Have you ever heard anything that Mary Connolly has said to the little one?

A. She said something to me. I told her once, "Why don't you let your little child out on the street and down in the yard? She says "I am afraid she will fall down on the stairs." and I say, "Mrs. Connolly I never saw a child like yours. Where is she when you go out?" And she says, "She is home." I says, "I never saw a child so still as that; I did not hear her all day." And she said, "Well the reason is when I went out I went in the church and I put her in the bed room." And I says, "You didn't lock your bedroom?" And she says "My husband, he makes a hook on it."

Q. Did you ever speak to her about whipping her child?

A. No sir, she told me once, that little child here is the devil. She tells everything to her father when he comes home; if she got something to eat for her alone, or she got some company and she got a little bit, she told everything to her father, and that makes her so mad. She knows more than a girl ten or eleven years old.

Q. Is this all you know about it?

A. Yes, sir. I hear her lying in that corner. I told my husband that I heard that little child every night; I guess she sleeps in that corner, and I saw her lying there once the first night she moved in; I saw her in the morning; the door was open and she lay in that corner, and I think she lies all the time in that corner on the floor.

Q. Do you ever hear the child crying in the night?

A. No, she did not cry; she is afraid. When the woman is not home, when she is alone you would never think there is a child in there.

249

Q.	And every morning you hear it in there?
A.	Every morning I hear it; and she hollers, "mamma."

The foregoing deposition having been	)
reduced to writing and having been	)
read by me to the said Mary Smitts	)
was on this 11th day of April 1874	)
by her enscribed and sworn to before me.	)

Mary (X) Smitt

Francis Lynde Stetson
Referee

NEW YORK SUPREME COURT
In the matter of the	)
Custody of a child	)
called Mary Ellen	)

Before Hon. A. R. Lawrence
Justice of the Supreme Court

New York, April 13, 1874

<u>Mrs. Mary Webb,</u> a witness produced being by me duly sworn testified as follows:

By Mr. Gerry

Q.	Where do you reside?
A.	Police Head Quarters; I am Matron of Police Head Quarters.

Q. What is your official connection with that establishment?

A. To see to the children that are brought in.

Q. The stray children which are found wandering about the city are brought by the police to head-quarters and consigned to your care?

A. Yes, sir.

Q. And kept there until claimed or otherwise disposed of?

A. Yes, sir.

Q. Have you seen the child Mary Ellen?

A. I have sir.

Q. Do you remember when she was first brought to head-quarters?

A. I do.

Q. When was it?

A. I think it was the evening of the 9th.

Q. I want you to state what the condition of the child was in regard to clothing, and further whether you made any examination of her, and what her condition was as regards cleanliness, and also whether you found any marks or scars, or bruises of any description upon her. Just go on, will you please and describe what you then saw?

A. In the first place her clothing was in very bad condition and very dirty. I took them off of her and found her body in the same condition. It was dirty not from a week's standing or a month but I should suppose for months, because it was crusted on like a child that had not been washed for months – the body of the child.

Q. Was this dirt plainly visible?

A. Yes, indeed it was; as it was washed off it left a thick scum over the bath.

Q. So that it required some washing to remove it?

A.   Yes, sir, it did.

Q.   What did you use in order to get rid of it?

A.   Plenty of soap and warm water.

Q.   How many washings did it require in order to remove the whole of this deposit of dirt upon the skin?

A.   Three different waters were applied to the child.

Q.   Was this universally the condition of the surface of the body underneath the clothing?

A.   Yes, sir. The feet also – she had never run on the street with bare feet but they were discolored like children who run in the house with bare feet. They were bluish and no dark dirt on them that a child would get by running out. She had three distinct bruises on her and others.

Q.   Where was the first of these bruises?

A.   One was just above the hip and one just above the elbow, and another a little above the left knee. One was as if very recently done.

Q.   Which was that?

A.   The one just above the elbow was very plain, and dark as if very recently done, but the others looked as though they had been done some little time previous so that they were disappearing.

Q.   You are familiar of course, from having seen a large number of these children, with the condition of the feet, are you not, when they are brought in?

A.   Yes, sir.

Q.   And you can determine from the general appearance of the feet of the child as to whether it has been in the habit of running in the street or not?

A.   Yes, sir. This child had not the appearance of running in the street.

Q.   You can tell by looking at the child's feet?

A.   Yes, sir.

Q.   How long have you been in charge of this department?

A.   Two years next August.

Q.   How many children during that time have been brought to your notice within the department?

A.   In warm weather we average 300 a month. In the month of May we have had 400, but the other months they vary.

Q.   You have had a large experience then with children?

A.   Yes, sir.

Q.   What was the condition of this child's hair?

A.   It was very bad; I had it combed. Of course there was vermin in it.

Q.   The hair was full of vermin, was it?

A.   I cannot say exactly full. I have had children come in with much more, but still it was too much for any child that has any care.

Q.   Did it present the appearance of having been combed for any recent time?

A.   Well the head seemed to be clean; the little thing said that the mother used to make her wash her own head; that was all the attention it got – every morning, but then it was not combed, I don't think.

Q.   All the attention that the head got was by her own washing?

A.   I asked her if anyone combed her head and she said no, but her mother made her wash her head every morning but I guess it got no combing; it could not have, or it would not have had vermin in it.

Q.   Did she say wash her face or her hair?

A.   She said her head, I questioned her about it. I suppose she meant the head and hair both.

Q.   Did you observe any scars or marks upon the face?

A.   The first day I saw her she had a very dark purple spot right on the forehead and side and a large scratch which was done with the scissors and another mark with a whip on the temple.

Q.   Did she so state?

A.   She said that the mark was done with a whip and the scratch was done with the scissors.

Q.   And those marks were plainly visible when you first saw her?

A.   When I got her they were plain but now we have washed her and cleansed her and fussed with her until they have quite disappeared; they don't show much now.

Q.   The clothes that she has on today when she is produced here in court are not the clothes with which she was clothed then?

A.   No sir, not one article.

Q.   They have been placed on her since?

A.   Yes, sir. I had them put on her.

17

Testimony of George Kellock

NEW YORK SUPREME COURT
In the matter of the   )
Custody of a child   )
called Mary Ellen   )

Before Hon. A. R. Lawrence
Justice of the Supreme Court

New York, April 13, 1874

<u>George Kellock,</u> a witness produced being by me duly
sworn testified:

<u>By Mr. Gerry</u>

Q.   What official position do you hold if any in
      connection with any of our institutions?
A.   Superintendent of Out Door Poor.
Q.   In what department?
A.   Public Charities and Correction.

Q.   How long have you occupied that position?

A.   Since 1848.

Q.   Do you know this woman, Mary Connolly?

A.   I cannot say that I do know her, sir.

Q.   Have you been able to find anything and if so will you kindly give us any information which you have been enabled to derive from the records in your office in regard to this child called Mary Ellen, and who is mentioned under the name of Mary Ellen Wilson in an indenture purporting to come from your office and signed by you as one of the parties to it.

A.   Yes, sir (producing a book).

Q.   What book is that?

A.   Nurse Book No. 15, folio 58 1/2.

Q.   What do you find there?

A.   "Mary Ellen Wilson 18 mo. old, left in charge of deponent about the 21st of May, 1864. Has received $8 per month until three weeks since. Does not know where the mother lives. As per affidavit of Mary Score No.235 Mulberry Street, July 7, 1865. (signed) Almshouse B. Island, July 10, 1865."

Q.   I observe on the right hand of the entry the words "Almshouse B. Island July 10, 1865." What does that mean?

A.   It means that she was sent up there to nurse at the time she was brought to the Department.

Q.   The words "Mary Ellen Wilson 18 mo." Does that mean eighteen months at the time this entry was made?

A.   Eighteen months old; yes, sir.

Q.   About what time was this entry made?

A.   The date is there.

Q.   At the bottom?

A.   Yes, sir.

Q.   July 7, 1865?

A.   Yes, sir.

Q.   Is that right?

A.   Yes, sir.

Q.   Have you been able to find any affidavit of Mary Score No. 235 Mulberry Street?

A.   We have not. We have moved our office since that time and the affidavits previous to 1870 are perhaps somewhere about the building but we cannot lay our hands on them at present.

Q.   I wish you would kindly make another diligent search if you will.

A.   I will.

Q.   I would like to get at who the notary was who took the affidavit?

A.   It was before the magistrate. We don't take them unless they go before a magistrate.

Q.   Is there any other record of that indenture required to be had anywhere by the regulations of the Department or by the rules which are established?

A.   I don't know whether the magistrate at the Tombs has it. He might have it there. I think the affidavit was made at the Tombs.

Q.   In regard to the mention here, "Has received $8 per month until three weeks since", have you any clue as to where that memorandum comes from as to whom that $8 was paid by? Is that paid by the Department?

A.   That is paid by the party who placed the child in care of Mary Score but neglected to keep up paying for it I presume; she gave it to us.

Q.   Do you know who Mary Score is?

A.   I do not.

Q.   She is not a nurse or any person connected in any way with your Department?

A.   No, sir.

Q.   From this entry and your familiarity with the books and the way in which these records were kept what does this indicate, "Affidavit of Mary Score No.235 Mulberry Street." Would that be the party who took the child?

A.   That would be the residence of the party making the affidavit.

Q.   This affidavit, as I understand you, does not appear to be that of the mother?

A.   No, it is the affidavit of the person in charge of the child, Mary Score.

Q.   And do I understand from this that she is a person who had some official charge of the child through your Department.

A.   No, sir.

Q.   Some person who had charge of the child before she came to you.

A.   Some person who had charge before it came to us.

Q.   After this affidavit was made, the child, as I understand, was sent up to Blackwell's Island?

A.   Yes, sir.

Q.   And kept in the Almshouse until called out by these people?

A.   Yes, sir.

Q.   In regard to the application by these people for this child, before making that application were they bound either to give a bond or make an affidavit or enter into any undertaking?

A.   No, sir, they being merely a reference in regard to their capability of taking care of the child.

Q.   Do you remember the reference they gave you?

A.   I do not remember, but I think it was Dr. McLachlan.

Q.   She referred them to this Dr. McLachlan?

A.   He was her family physician at that time.

Q.   Did you know this Dr. McLachlan?

A.   I think I did from what she said about it.

Q.   Can you tell me where he can be found?

A.   I think I can find him.

Q.   Was the deposit of the child under that indenture which she has produced in court, and which I believe you have a duplicate of in your books?

A.   Yes, sir.

Q.   Was the deposit of that child made on the representations of Dr. McLachlan that the woman was a competent person?

A.   Yes, sir. that the woman and the man both were competent to take care of the child.

Q.   They were both parties to the agreement?

A.   Yes, sir.

Q.   Did they specify this particular child? How did they come to select this child? Do you remember?

A.   I do not, but the general way is they go and look among the children and pick out one they think will suit and then they come down to me to get an order for the child.

Q.   Then the first thing this woman must have done before she got this child was to have gone to the Department Almshouse at Blackwell's Island and asked to see the child called Mary Ellen Wilson?

A.   I don't think so; I think she saw all the children.

Q.   There would have been a record at Blackwell's Island containing the name of this child?

A.   Yes, sir a facsimile of that.

Q.   A facsimile of this copy then was transmitted to the Almshouse at Blackwell's Island with the child?

A.   I don't say a facsimile. The name and the age and the folio and the book; not the affidavit or anything of that kind.

Q.   I understand that, but there was a record of the name of the child as it appears here and the fact as to where it came from, with reference to the folio here?

A.   Yes, sir.

Q.   So that the child could be traced by anyone who knew the child and wanted to find out what became of it?

A.   Yes, sir.

Q.   That could be done?

A.   That could be done, yes, sir.

Q.   Then she could have found out the name of the child at the Almshouse?

A.   Yes, sir.

Q.   And without seeing the child?

A.   Yes, sir.

Q.   At the Almshouse do they permit people to see children without a permit?

A.   No, sir.

Q.   A permit from whom?

A.   From me.

Q.   Do you remember having given any permit to this woman to go and see the child?

A.   No, sir, I don't remember, I presume I did.

Q.   I suppose you have so many that it is almost impossible to recollect any particular one?

A.   Yes, sir.

Q.   She could not visit the child there without a permit?

A.   No, sir.

Q.   Have you any present recollection of this woman having applied to you for any such permit?

A.   I have a recollection of seeing her before but I cannot place it exactly in my mind to testify about it.

Q.   Who is the person who signed his name on the indenture of which you have a copy, as the witness of it?

A.   Mr. Boswell, he was one of the clerks in the office.

Q.   Is he there with you now?

A.   Yes, sir.

Q.   After seeing the child up at Blackwell's Island the next course then is an application to you for an indenture, is it?

A.   For an order to get it.

Q.   Is the child brought down first before the indenture is given?

A.   No, sir, if the child is one that can be placed out and the reference is satisfactory the order is given to the party to obtain the child.

Q.   Without any indenture being made?

A.   The indenture is made after they have the child.

Q.   They are allowed to have the child first on the simple order?

A.   Yes, sir.

Q.   What is the form of that order?

A.   That the warden of the Almshouse will deliver such and such a child to the parties, mentioning their names and where they live.

Q.   Is the application required to be fortified by any affidavit?

A.   No affidavit, only the reference.

Q.   On being satisfied of the capacity of the party to take the child?

A.   If the reference is not satisfactory we generally send a visitor to look into the standing of the parties.

Q.   Your recollection is that in the present case the reference was satisfactory?

A.   I think the reference was satisfactory, he being a family physician.

Q.   You relied on the statement of the family physician as knowing more about the person than other persons?

A.   Yes, sir.

Q.   And you thought the physician was a man of good standing at the time?

A.   Yes, sir.

Q.   You had no supposition at all of any intention on the part of this woman to ill treat the child?

A.   Not the least.

Q.   And you knew nothing about the story that she has told as to its being an illegitimate child of her husband?

A.   No, sir.

Q.   Was any such notice or information conveyed to you?

A.   Not in the least, until I saw it conveyed in the papers.

Q.   That is the first you heard of it?

A.   Yes, sir.

Q.   Did the husband of this woman, Mr. McCormick the former husband, who united with her in this – did he make any statement about the child being his?

A.   Nothing of the kind.

Q.   Did she make any statement about what she wanted the child for?

A.   Nothing of the kind to my knowledge.

Q.   Do you find any other entry of the name of Wilson or any other child of the name of Wilson about that time?

A.   No, sir.

Q.   Who is the person at the almshouse that would have charge of the child while there?

A. The person who was in charge of the almshouse at that time is not there now.

Q. Can you give me his name?

A. I don't remember. I think I can obtain it for you. Of course I can find out who it is.

Q. I will thank you if you will. Do they keep a report at the almshouse similar to this?

A. Yes, sir.

Q. And that would show the disposition of the child on the order?

A. Yes, sir.

Q. So as to fix the date when she actually got the child?

A. Yes, sir.

Q. Who is the person at the almshouse who has charge of that?

A. Mr. Vought, but he does not have the children up there. We have a separate place for them now.

Q. I mean the record?

A. The record is at the almshouse.

Q. And Mr. Vought has charge of it?

A. Yes, sir.

Q. Do you know his first name?

A. No.

Q. Do you remember of any other person having called at any time to see the child?

A. No, sir.

Q. Or apply for the child?

A. No, sir.

Q. Either before or subsequent, up to the time when you saw me about the matter the other day?

A. No, sir.

Q. No such application?

A. No such application. We were then looking up the history of it when you came in.

Q. You saw it in the paper?

263

A.   Yes, sir.

Q.   What I wanted to get at was whether any person had exhibited any interest in the child from the time this woman applied for it up to the present time?

A.   No, sir. I have no knowledge of it.

Q.   The indenture requires that she shall report each year as to the condition of the child. I want to ask you first how is the report made; is it a report in writing or does she bring the child?

A.   They generally bring the child and show it to the Department.

Q.   Who does she show it to?

A.   Shows it to me, or the Commissioners if they are there.

Q.   Do you remember her bringing the child?

A.   I think I saw her bring it once or twice.

Q.   I want to ask you what was the condition of that child as to her manner of clothing, and her condition in regard to cleanliness and on the occasions when you think she produced the child before you. Can you bear in mind anything about it?

A.   I don't remember any child being produced there that was not clothed pretty well, and looked pretty well when it was brought there. I would have noticed the difference of course.

Q.   How many children do you have passing through your establishment every year?

A.   A great many.

Q.   Can you give me any idea of it?

A.   Perhaps 500 or 600 a year.

Q.   Of course you don't bear in mind the appearance of any particular child?

A.   No, sir.

Q. Was there anything in the child's appearance when she was produced before you that you remember now that attracted your attention in any way?

A. No, sir.

Q. It was just in a formal way?

A. Yes, sir.

Q. Did you ever have any conversation with this Dr. McLachlan about the child?

A. No, sir.

Q. Since that time when he certified as to the correctness of the woman's deportment on which you say you gave her the child you have not seen him?

A. No, sir. I may have seen him but I don't remember.

Q. He did not speak to you about the child?

A. No, sir, nothing to call my attention.

Q. Can you give me the address of Dr. McLachlan?

A. No, sir.

Q. Do you know his first name?

A. No, sir. I can obtain it for you.

Q. Do you know where he lived at that time?

A. I think he lived somewhere in the neighborhood of 23rd Street although I am not positive – 23rd St. near Third Avenue.

Q. Do your rules require you to keep any particular memorandum in regard to the presentation of these children as required by that indenture?

A. Well we do not do it. They generally bring them to us and report; some of the reports we have received in writing. Those we keep on file.

Q. This was not one of those cases?

A. No, sir.

Q. There is no report in writing in reference to this child?

A. No sir, she brought the child to the office in person.

Q. Did you have any conversation with the child at any time?

A. Sometimes I do.

Q. Do you remember having any with this one?

A. No, sir.

Q. Excuse me for being so particular; I want to search it out and see if there is anything which remains in the matter. The office was in Bond St. was it not where this transfer must have taken place?

A. Yes, sir.

Is there any security required to be given on the indenture.

A. No, sir, no security only character, that is all.

Q. I mean pecuniary security?

A. No, sir.

Q. Can you give me in any way any trace to this woman Mary Score. Do you know whether she had charge of any other children?

A. No, sir. I do not.

Q. Is there anything else that I can ask you?

A. I don't know of anything else. I would be glad to give you any information I could.

18

Testimony of Martha Score

NEW YORK SUPREME COURT
In the matter of the   )
Custody of a child   )
called Mary Ellen   )

Before Hon. A. R. Lawrence
Justice of the Supreme Court

New York, April 21, 1874

<u>Martha Score,</u> a witness produced being by me duly
sworn testified as follows:

     <u>By Mr. Gerry</u>

Q.   What is your name.
A.   Martha Score.
Q.   Are you married or single?
A.   Married.
Q.   What is the name of your husband?

A.   James Score.

Q.   What is his business?

A.   He is a cigar maker.

Q.   Where do you reside now?

A.   195 Mulberry Street.

Q.   Do you remember anything about a child called Mary Ellen Wilson that was delivered by you into the custody of the Commissioner of Charities and Corrections, some years since?

A.   Yes, sir I took care of her for her mother; at least she told me she was her mother; for $2. a week.

Q.   How did she come to come to you?

A.   By an acquaintance.

Q.   Had you known her previously?

A.   No, sir, I never was acquainted with her.

Q.   Who was the acquaintance that brought her mother to you?

A.   She was living in the house I did.

Q.   What was her name?

A.   Mrs. Cavanagh.

Q.   Spelled with a "C" or a "K"?"

A.   I don't know.

Q.   She lived in the same house with you then?

A.   No, sir, not in the same house with me at that time, but she was a neighbor.

Q.   She had previously lived in the same house?

A.   Yes, sir.

Q.   Were you married at that time?

A.   Yes, sir.

Q.   Had you children of your own?

A.   Yes, sir, three.

Q.   And this Mrs. Cavanagh, what did she say about this woman, before she came to you?

A.   She told me she was a servant in the St. Nicholas Hotel. She asked me if I would take care of this baby for her, she had no person to take care of it and she would pay me, and I done so as my husband was away and it would help me along.

Q. Did she say what place she occupied in the St. Nicholas Hotel as a servant?

A. Cake baker.

Q. What did she say the name of this woman was, the mother of the child?

A. Fannie Wilson.

Q. Do you know whether she said anything about the parentage of the child?

A. No, sir.

Q. Did she say anything about Fannie Wilson being married or single?

A. She told me she was a married woman and her husband was in the war and her husband died and she was a widow woman.

Q. Did she say anything whatever, about this child being her own or an illegitimate child?

A. Her own child she told me.

Q. You saw this Fannie Wilson?

Q. What sort of a person was she?

A. A good looking woman, dark eyes and dark hair.

Q. Was she tall?

A. Medium size.

Q. She was a good looking woman?

A. Very good looking.

Q. How old a woman was she?

A. I could not tell you.

Q. About how old?

A. About 30 years, not quite; from 27 to 30, as near as I should judge.

Q. Have you any idea of what nationality she was, whether Irish or American?

A. She told me she was an English woman.

Q. Did she say anything about what the name of her husband was?

A. She has told me but I forget.

Q. Did she say what position he occupied in the army?

A. No, sir.

Q. Or in what regiment?

A. In Billy Wilson's Corps.

Q. And he was killed down South?

A. So she said.

Q. Before she came to you?

A. Yes, sir.

Q. At the time she came to you, this Fannie Wilson, did she say what business she was in?

A. She told me she was working at the St. Nicholas Hotel.

Q. Did she tell you in what capacity she was working there?

A. Cake baker.

Q. Did she tell you how long she had been there?

Q. What reason did she give for putting the child with you?

A. That is more than I can tell.

Q. Did she give any reason?

A. No, sir.

Q. What did she ask you about it?

A. She asked me if I would take care of it and she would pay me.

Q. Did she give you any clothing with the child?

A. A few little articles, not a great deal.

Q. How much a week did she give you?

A. $2.

Q. Won't you fix the time as near as you can, about the time when she first gave you that child?

A.   I really could not say. I should think it was about a year after my husband – I could not say. I really could not say.

Q.   Could you fix that date as near as possible?

A.   I really could not say.

Q.   About how old was the child when she was brought to you?

A.   Between five and six months.

Q.   Was it as long ago as ten years?

A.   No, sir, it is not.

Q.   Not as long as ten years?

A.   I could not say exactly.

Q.   You made an application - you resided at 235 Mulberry Street in 1865.

A.   Yes, sir.

Q.   It appears by the entries which have been produced here in evidence by the Commissioners of Charities and Corrections, Mr. Kellock, you know him personally, don't you?

A.   Yes, sir.

Q.   That on the 7th of July 1865, Mary Ellen Wilson months old, left in charge of deponent about the 21st of May 1864, has received $8 per month, until three weeks since; does not know where the mother lives, as per affidavit of Mary Score5 Mulberry Street. You made such an affidavit?

A.   Yes, sir.

Q.   Was that date accurate, about the 21st of May 16, 1864? The entry here is that you stated that Mary Ellen Wilson was 18 months old and was living with you about the 21st of May 1864?

A.   I could not say.

Q.   But the affidavit you made at that time, stated the date correctly didn't it.

A.   I guess so.

271

Q. How long did you keep the child before you delivered her up to the Commissioners of Charities and Corrections?

A. About a year.

Q. And up to that time, was the money paid by this woman, $2. a week?

A. While she lived in the St. Nicholas, she paid me $2. a week for the child punctually; then she went away and I could not get any trace of her for some time. I went to this Mrs. Cavanagh to see if she knew anything about her. I went up with her and found Mrs. Wilson there.

Q. Where?

A. Up at the corner of 7th Street an 3rd Avenue, where the relief was given.

Q. What relief?

A. From the Soldiers Relief; then she gave me the ticket to draw the money to pay for the baby; then I didn't see anything of her.

Q. Do you recollect the name of the soldier who was on that ticket?

A. No, sir, I do not.

Q. When was the last that you ever saw this Mrs. Wilson?

A. I could not say.

Q. Have you got the ticket yet?

A. No, sir, the ticket was kept where the money was given.

Q. Have you any letter from her of any kind?

A. No, sir.

Q. Did she say who the father of the child was?

A. She told me Mr. Wilson; he was in the war, that is all I know.

Q. Did she say what business her husband was in before he went to the war?

A.   She told me he was an oyster man in the St. Nicholas.

Q.   Did she say anything about the place where he was killed?

A.   No, sir.

Q.   Do you know where she is now; have you ever heard of her since?

A.   No, sir.

Q.   Did she ever call on you or write to you afterwards?

A.   I seen her afterwards and told her about the child and she told me the child was all right.

Q.   Where did you see her?

A.   I met her accidentally on the sidewalk.

Q.   How long after that, was it that you gave up the child.

A.   I could not say how long; it is so long ago.

Q.   Was it a year?

A.   I could not say.

Q.   Excepting that occasion, have you ever seen her since?

A.   No, sir.

Q.   When did Mrs. Cavanagh die?

A.   I think it was last summer.

Q.   Did this woman, Fannie Wilson at any time go to Blackwell's Island with the child that you know of?

A.   No, sir, I never did know.

Q.   Did she appear to be attached to the child?

A.   She used to come and see her and then go away to work.

Q.   Was the child a nursing child when you took it?

Q.   Was it a nursing child when you took it?

A.   No, sir.

Q.   Did the mother appear to exhibit any symptoms of affection when she came to see her?

A.   Yes, sir.

273

Q.   Did she kiss the child?

A.   Yes, sir.

Q.   Did she say to you where she got the money from that she paid you, while the child was with you?

A.   No, sir, she did not.

Q.   Did she give any reason for stopping the payment of the money?

A.   She did not stop, she left the St. Nicholas at that time.

Q.   Then she paid for the child out of her wages?

A.   Yes, sir, for sometime.

Q.   Have you any idea of any means by which we can ascertain the whereabouts of this Fannie Wilson?

A.   No, sir.

Q.   Do you know anyone that knows her in any way?

A.   No, sir.

Q.   How long is it since you heard from her or of her?

A.   I could not say.

Q.   Several years?

A.   A good many years it must be.

Q.   Have you been up to the Police Headquarters and seen the child Mary Ellen?

A.   Yes, sir.

Q.   Does she look like the same child?

A.   As near as I could judge.

Q.   The child was kindly treated so long as she remained with you?

A.   I didn't treat her bad.

Q.   You treated her the same as your own children?

A.   The same as my own.

Q.   How large an amount was there on this relief ticket that you say you drew?

A. $4. every two weeks.

Q.   Did she give you the whole of it for the child?

A. $4. every two weeks.

Q.   That was the whole amount that she was entitled to on the ticket at the time?

A.   Yes, sir, that is all.

Q.   How long a time did that continue?

A.   I could not say.

Q.   It was nearly a year wasn't it?

A.   No, sir.

Q.   Did she always pay you the money in that way?

A.   No, sir, she didn't. While she lived in the St. Nicholas, she paid me – she drew the money and paid me – when she left the St. Nicholas, she went away and I didn't hear anything of her for some time and I hunted her up again and she gave me the ticket.

Q.   How did you hunt her up?

A.   I went to this Mrs. Cavanagh.

Q.   Is Mrs. Cavanagh's husband alive?

A.   She has been a widow for sometime.

Q.   Has she any children living?

A.   She has one.

Q.   What is the name of the child?

A.   Bridget.

Q.   Where is she to be found?

A.   I don't know.

Q.   Have you any idea where she is to be found?

A.   I have no idea where she is.

Q.   How old a person is Bridget Cavanagh, the daughter of your friend?

A.   I don't know.

Q.   About how old should you judge her to be?

A.   She is a married woman.

Q.   Do you know her other name?

A.   No, sir, I do not.

Q.   Did you ever see her with Fannie Wilson at all?

A.   No, sir, I never did.

275

Q.   Mr. Hawk kept the St. Nicholas at that time didn't he?

A.   I don't know who kept it.

Q.   Do you know anyone else that knows this Fannie Wilson?

A.   No, sir, I do not.

Q.   Did you ever hear of Mrs. Connolly applying to take this child from the Commissioners of Charities and Corrections?

A.   No, sir, I don't know anything about it; the first I seen was in the papers.

Q.   Where did you find Fannie Wilson after she left the St. Nicholas. You say Mrs. Cavanagh told you where to find her; where was she staying then?

A.   I could not say.

Q.   Can you remember?

A.   No, sir, she didn't tell me where she was stopping.

Q.   Did Mrs. Cavanagh bring her and you together?

A.   Mrs. Cavanagh and me found her up where they were drawing the relief; there is where we found her. She didn't tell me where she was stopping or anything.

Q.   Do you remember whether the name on the red ticket which you gave in at the Soldiers Relief, when you got the money, had the same name on it as the name of the child – the name of Wilson?

A.   I didn't take any notice, and even it is so long ago that I could not remember even if I did take notice at that time.

19

Where To Put The Child?

When Mary Ellen was removed from the Connolly home, Judge Lawrence committed her to an institution called "Sheltering Arms". Here is the order, transcribed from a handwritten copy:

> Before
> Abraham R. Lawrence, Esq.,
> A Justice of the Supreme Court
> Of The State of New York at
> The City Hall in the City of
> New York

In the Matter of the	)
Custody of a Child	)
Called Mary Ellen	)

Upon reading and filing the petition of Henry Bergh in the above proceeding verified April 9th, 1874, and on all the proceedings had thereabouts together with the testimony taken in any part of the allegations contained in said petition; and it appearing to my satisfaction that all the material allegations in said petition are true and that the said child Mary Ellen has been cruelly and wantonly ill treated, beaten, assaulted and bruised by her former custodian the said Mary Connolly; and that the said Mary Connolly is a wholly unfit and improper person to have the further custody and control of said child; and that if said custody and control should be continued it would result in irreparable damage and injury to said child Mary Ellen. [Illegible] Statute in such case made and provided and of the power in me vested, I do hereby order that the said child Mary Ellen be released , discharged, and taken from the custody and control of the said Mary Connolly, and committed to the care and custody of the Managers of the institution known as the "Sheltering Arms" located at the City of New York, there to be and remain until the further order of the Supreme Court or until the said child Mary Ellen shall attain the age of twenty one years.

Witness my hand and seal this 30th Day of December, 1874
(signed) Abm. R. Lawrence
Justice of the Supreme Court

Etta Wheeler was concerned about Lawrence's decision to send Mary Ellen to the Sheltering Arms facility. It was not a place for young girls, but a home for prostitutes, thieves, and runaways. Mary Ellen was an innocent victim who bore no responsibility for her dire situation. Etta wrote to Bergh and Judge Lawrence, appealing to them to place Mary Ellen elsewhere. Eventually, Judge Lawrence, her official guardian, did that with the following order:

> Before Abraham R. Lawrence, Esq., A Justice of the Supreme Court Of The State of New York at The City Hall in the City of New York

In the Matter of the	)
Custody of a Child	)
Called Mary Ellen	)

Whereas by an order made and entered herein on the 30th day of December, 1874, the said child Mary Ellen was committed to the care and custody of the Managers of the institution known as the "Sheltering Arms" located at the City of New York, there to be and remain until the further order of the Supreme Court and it now appearing to my satisfaction that the future welfare of the said child will be better promoted by removing her from said custody, now therefore, I do hereby order that the said child be taken from the custody of said institution and committed to the custody and control of the Managers of the Institution known as "The Woman's Aid Society and Home for Friendless Girls" located at the City of New York, there to be and remain until the further order of the Supreme Court or until the said child Mary Ellen shall attain the age of twenty one years.

Witness my hand and seal this Second day of March75

(signed) Abm. R. Lawrence, Justice of the Supreme Court

While this was the result for which Etta was appealing, it was not the ultimate result she desired. She appealed continuously throughout Mary Ellen's confinement at both the Sheltering Arms and the Woman's Aid Society and Home for Friendless Girls for Mary Ellen to be placed with her sister and brother-in-law, Elizabeth and Darius Spencer just outside Rochester. Clearly, Etta knew the judge's reasons for the delay; he was reviewing several custody appeals from family members both in the United States and in England, including from her grandparents, Michael and Mary Connor.

After almost an entire year, Henry Bergh penned the following appeal to Judge Lawrence:

June 4th75

Honorable Abraham R. Lawrence

Dear Sir,

> Mrs. Wheeler, the excellent lady who was instrumental in aiding me in rescuing "little Mary Ellen" from the hands of a brutal woman, has called to see me in relation to procuring her a home with her sister, who resides near Rochester in this state.
> I take the liberty to address you on the subject, for the purpose of assuring you that no better disposition of that child could possibly be made. Mrs. Wheeler is a most amiable, intelligent, and Christian lady, and her sister is like her. The Matron of the establishment where she is at

present, and all others familiar with the locality and her surroundings, are unanimous in the opinion that she should be removed without delay.

With Mrs. Wheeler's sister, she would have a good home, and be returned to morality and usefulness aloof from the vices of a great city.

I earnestly and most sincerely hope that you will sanction this proposal on the part of these ladies and issue an order to that effect so that she may accompany Mrs. Wheeler to the country on Monday next, when she is obliged to leave, owing to the illness of her mother. If possible will you please return a reply by the bearer?

And believe me,
   Your most obedient Servant,
     Henry Bergh

The request was almost immediately granted. Less than a month later, Etta reported back to Henry Bergh on Mary Ellen's progress. Here is the letter:

New York, June 2475

My Dear Mr. Bergh,

I returned to the city yesterday, leaving Mary Ellen very contentedly domiciled with my sister.

The child bears the freedom and variety of her new life with much good sense, but with a very keen enjoyment. For the first time in her life, she is unrestrained by bolts and locks, and she enjoys being out-of-doors as an escaped soul would Paradise. She is still a bit shy of all the household pets, the babies excepted, but they were all making love to her, insisting upon being friends, and she was fast losing her terror. She was greatly troubled by my coming away, but seems already quite attached to my sister and her family. She is a helpful, kindhearted little creature and is making friends for herself.

Her ignorance of the ordinary affairs of home life, and of the commonest objects in the country amused as well as pained us. She was very kindly received by all my friends and not alone for my sake, but for her own. I expended of the twenty-five dollars sent by yourself — traveling expenses and necessary clothing were sixteen dollars, I gave my sister four dollars, and the remaining five dollars is to be put in the bank for Mary Ellen's benefit. She will, if well, earn her clothes hereafter, in her ready way of helping in household affairs.

With thanks for your kindness,
I am very truly,
Mrs. C. C. Wheeler
122 W. 45th St.

20

Children of The Poor

Jacob Riis (1849-1914) was in court the day Mary Ellen was carried in. His poignant photography depicting the conditions of poverty in which so many people lived brought awareness to those who had no idea such conditions existed.

Jacob Riis arrived in America when he was 21, emigrating from Denmark. Life here was not easy, and he struggled until securing work as a police court reporter for the New York Tribune.

Riis was very concerned with social conditions, particularly in the tenements of New York City, and this is where he focused his attentions. His first book, "How the Other Half Lives", exposed the tragic conditions to the world, and to one man in particular. One day, Riis returned to his office to find a note on his desk that read, "I have read your book and I have come to help." It was from none other than the head of the New York Police Board of Commissioners, Theodore Roosevelt – later to become a US president. He was affected by the photographs taken by Riis, and was instrumental in securing a number of reforms.

The following chapter is directly from his book, "Children of the Poor", published in 1892. In it, he speaks about the Mary Ellen rescue and her life afterward, as well as how the case affected change throughout the country.

Here is Chapter IX of "Children of the Poor":

CHAPTER IX.
Little Mary Ellen's Legacy

On a thriving farm up in Central New York a happy young wife goes singing about her household work to-day who once as a helpless, wretched waif in the great city through her very helplessness and misery stirred up a social revolution whose waves beat literally upon the farthest shores. The story of little Mary Ellen moved New York eighteen years ago as it had scarce ever been stirred by news of disaster or distress before. In the simple but eloquent language of the public record it is thus told: "In the summer of 1874 a poor woman lay dying in the last stages of consumption in a miserable little room on the top floor of a big tenement in this city. A Methodist missionary, visiting among the poor, found her there and asked what she could do to soothe her sufferings. 'My time is short,' said the sick woman, 'but I cannot die in peace while the miserable little girl whom they call Mary Ellen is being beaten day and night by her stepmother next door to my room.' She told how the screams of the child were heard at all hours. She was locked in the room, she understood. It had been so for months, while she had been lying ill there. Prompted by the natural instinct of humanity, the missionary sought the aid of the police, but she was told that it was necessary to furnish evidence before an arrest could be made. 'Unless you can prove that an offence has been committed we cannot interfere, and all you know

Jacob Riis

is hearsay.' She next went to several benevolent societies in the city whose object it was to care for children, and asked their interference in behalf of the child. The reply was: 'If the child is legally brought to us, and is a proper subject, we will take it; otherwise we cannot act in the matter.' In turn then she consulted several excellent charitable citizens as to what she should do. They replied: 'It is a dangerous thing to interfere between parent and child, and you might get yourself into trouble if you did so, as parents are proverbially the best guardians of their own children.' Finally, in despair, with the piteous appeals of the dying woman ringing in her ears, she said: 'I will make one more effort to save this child. There is one man in this city who has never turned a deaf ear to the cry of the helpless and who has spent his life in just this work for the benefit of unoffending animals. I will go to Henry Bergh.'

"She went, and the great friend of the dumb brute found a way. 'The child is an animal,' he said, 'if there is no justice for it as a human being, it shall at least have the rights of the stray cur in the street. It shall not be abused.' And thus was written the first bill of rights for the friendless waif the world over. The appearance of the starved, half-naked, and bruised child when it was brought into court wrapped in a horse blanket caused a sensation that stirred the public conscience to its very depths. Complaints poured in upon Mr. Bergh; so many cases of child-beating and fiendish cruelty came to light in a little while, so many little savages were hauled forth from their dens of misery, that the community stood aghast. A meeting of citizens was called and an association for the defence of outraged childhood was formed, out of which grew the Society for the Prevention of Cruelty to Children that was formally incorporated in the following year. By that time Mary Ellen was safe in a good home. She never saw her tormentor again. The woman, whose name was Connolly, was not her mother. She steadily refused to tell where she got the child, and the mystery of its descent was never solved. The wretched woman was sent to the Island and forgotten.

John D. Wright, a venerable Quaker merchant, was chosen the first President of the Society. Upon the original call for the first meeting, preserved in the archives of the Society, may still be read a foot-note in his handwriting, quaintly amending the date to read, Quaker fashion, "12th mo. 15th , 1874." A year

Mary Ellen Wilson, around age 15. (Courtesy of the George Sim Johnston Archives of the NYSPCC.)

later, in his first review of the work hat was before the young society, he wrote, "Ample laws have been passed by the Legislature of this State for the protection of and prevention of cruelty to little children. The trouble seems to be that it is nobody's business to enforce them. Existing societies have as much, nay more to do than they can attend to in providing for those entrusted to their care. The Society for the Prevention of Cruelty to Children proposes to enforce by lawful means and with energy those laws, not vindictively, not to gain public applause,

but to convince those who cruelly ill-treat and shamefully neglect little children that the time has passed when this can be done, in this State at least, with impunity."

The promise has been faithfully kept. The old Quaker is dead, but his work goes on. The good that he did lives after him, and will live forever. The applause of the crowd his Society has not always won; but it has merited the confidence and approval of all right-thinking and right-feeling men. Its aggressive advocacy of defenceless childhood, always and everywhere, is to-day reflected from the statute-books of every State in the American Union, and well-nigh every civilized government abroad, in laws that sprang directly from its fearless crusade.

In theory it had always been the duty of the State to protect the child "in person, and property, and in its opportunity for life, liberty, and happiness," even against a worthless parent; in practice it held to the convenient view that, after all, the parent had the first right to the child and knew what was best for it. The result in many cases was thus described in the tenth annual report of the Society by President Elbridge T. Gerry, who in 1879 had succeeded Mr. Wright and has ever since been so closely identified with its work that it is as often spoken of nowadays as Mr. Gerry's Society as under its corporate name:

"Impecunious parents drove them from their miserable homes at all hours of the day and night to beg and steal. They were trained as acrobats at the risk of life and limb, and beaten cruelly if they failed. They were sent at night to procure liquor for parents too drunk to venture themselves into the streets. They were drilled in juvenile operas and song-and-dance variety business until their voices were cracked, their growth stunted, and their health permanently ruined by exposure and want of rest. Numbers of young Italians were imported by *padroni* under promises of a speedy return, and then sent out on the streets to play on musical instruments to peddle flowers and small wares to the passers-by, and too often as a cover for immorality. Their surroundings were those of vice, profanity, and obscenity. Their only amusements were the dance-halls, the cheap theatres and museums, and the saloons. Their acquaintances were those hardened in sin, and both boys and girls soon became adepts in crime, and entered unhesitatingly on the downward path. Beaten and abused at home, treated worse than animals, no other result could be expected. In the prisons, to which sooner or later these unhappy children gravitated, there was no separation of them from hardened criminals. Their previous education in vice rendered them apt scholars in the school of crime, and they ripened into criminals as they advanced in years."

All that has not been changed in the seventeen years that have passed; to remodel depraved human nature has been beyond the power of the Society; but step by step under its prompting the law has been changed and strengthened; step by step life has been breathed into its dead letter, until now it is as able and willing to protect the child against violence or absolute cruelty as the Society is to enforce its protection. There is work enough for it to do yet. I have outlined some in the preceding chapters. In the past year (1891) it investigated 7,695 complaints and rescued 3,683 children from pernicious surroundings, some of them from a worse fate than death. "But let it not be supposed from this," writes the Superintendent, "that crimes of and against children are on the increase. As a matter of fact wrongs to children have been materially lessened in New York by the Society's action and influence during the past seventeen years. Some have entirely disappeared, having been eradicated root and branch from New York life, and an influence for good has been felt by the children themselves, as shown by the great diminution in juvenile delinquency from 1875, when the Society was first organized, to 1891, the figures indicating a decrease of fully fifty per cent."[1]

Other charitable efforts, working along the same line, contributed their share, perhaps the greater, to the latter result, but the Society's influence upon the environment that shapes the childish mind and character, as well as upon the child itself, is undoubted. It is seen in the hot haste with which a general cleaning up and setting to rights is begun in a block of tenement barracks the moment the "cruelty man" heaves in sight; in the "holy horror" the child-beater has of him and his mission, and in the altered attitude of his victim, who not rarely nowadays confronts his tormentor with the threat, "if you do that I will go to the Children's Society," always effective except when drink blinds the wretch to consequences.

The Society had hardly been in existence four years when it came into collision with the padrone and his abominable system of child slavery. These

---

[1] Seventeenth Annual Report of Society92.

traders in human misery, adventurers of the worst type, made a practice of hiring the children of the poorest peasants in the Neapolitan mountain districts, to serve them begging, singing, and playing in the streets of American cities. The contract was for a term of years at the end of which they were to return the child and pay a fixed sum, a miserable pittance, to the parents for its use, but, practically, the bargain amounted to a sale, except that the money was never paid. The children left their homes never to return. They were shipped from Naples to Marseilles, and made to walk all the way through France, singing, playing, and dancing in the towns and villages through which they passed, to a seaport where they embarked for America. Upon their arrival here they were brought to a rendezvous in some out-of-the-way slum and taken in hand by the padrone, the partner of the one who had hired them abroad. He sent them out to play in the streets by day, singing and dancing in tune to their alleged music, and by night made them perform in the lowest dens in the city. All the money they made the padrone took from them, beating and starving them if they did not bring home enough. None of it ever reached their parents. Under this treatment the boys grew up thieves – the girls worse. The life soon wore them out, and the Potter's Field claimed them before their term of slavery was at an end, according to the contract. In far-off Italy the simple peasants waited anxiously for the return of little Tomaso or Antonia with the coveted American gold. No word ever came of them.

The vile traffic had been broken up in England only to be transferred to America. The

Italian government had protested. Congress had passed an act making it a felony for anyone knowingly to bring into the United States any person inveigled or forcibly kidnapped in any other country, with the intent to hold him here in involuntary service. But thee children were not only unable to either speak or understand English, they were compelled, under horrible threats, to tell anyone who asked that the padrone was their father, brother, or other near relative. To get the evidence upon which to proceed against the padrone was a task of exceeding difficulty, but it was finally accomplished by co-operation of the Italian government with the Society's agents in the case of the padrone Ancarola, who, in November79, brought over from Italy seven boy slaves, between nine and thirteen years old, with their outfit of harps and violins. They were seized, and the padrone, who escaped from the steamer, was arrested in a Crosby Street groggery five days later. Before a jury in the United States Court the whole vile scheme was laid bare. One of the boys testified that Ancarola had paid his mother 20 lire (about four dollars) and his uncle 60 lire. For this sum he was to serve the padrone four years.

Ancarola was convicted and sent to the penitentiary. The children were returned to their homes.

The news traveled slowly on the other side. For years the padrone's victims kept coming at intervals, but the society's agents were on the watch, and when the last of the kidnappers was sent to prison in 1885 there was an end of the business. The excitement attending the trial and the vigor with which the society had pushed its pursuit of the rascally padrone drew increased attention to its work. At the end of the following year twenty-four societies had been organized in other States upon its plan, and half the governments of Europe were enacting laws patterned after those of New York State. To-day there are a hundred societies for the prevention of cruelty to children in this country, independent of each other but owning the New York Society as their common parent, and nearly twice as many abroad, kin England, France, Italy, Spain, the West Indies, South America, Canada, Australia, etc. The old link that bound the dumb brute with the helpless child in a common bond of humane sympathy has never been broken. Many of them include both in their efforts, and all the American societies, whether their care be children or animals, are united in an association for annual conference and co-operation, called the American Humane Association.

In seventeen years the Society has investigated 61,749 complaints of cruelty to children, involving 185,247 children, prosecuted 21,282 offenders, and obtained 20,697 convictions. The children it has saved and released numbered at the end of the year 1891 no less than 32,633. Whenever it has been charged with erring it has been on the side of mercy for the helpless child. It follows its charges into the police courts, seeing to it that, if possible, no record of crime is made against the offending child and that it is placed at once where better environment may help bring out the better side of its nature. It follows them into the institutions to which they are committed through its care, and fights their battles there, if need be, or the battles of their guardians under the law, against the greed of parents that would sacrifice the child's prospects in life for the sake of the few pennies it could earn at home. And it generally wins the fight.

The Society has never received any financial support from the city, but has depended entirely upon private benevolence. Ample means have always been at its disposal. Last year it sheltered, fed, and clothes 1,697 children in its rooms. Most of them were the victims of drunken parents. With the Society they found safe shelter. "Sometimes," Superintendent Jenkins says, "the children cry when they are brought here. They always cry when they go away."

"Lastly," so ran the old Quaker merchant's address in his first annual report, "this Society, so far from interfering with the numerous societies and institutions already existing, is intended to aid them in their noble work. It proposes to labor in the interest of no one religious denomination, and to keep entirely free from political influences of every kind. Its duties toward the children whom it may rescue will be discharged when the future custody of them is decided by the courts of justice." Before the faithful adherence to that plan all factions or sectarian opposition that impedes and obstructs so many other charities has fallen away entirely. Humanity is the religion of the Children's Society. In its Board of Directors are men of all nationalities and of every creed. Its fundamental doctrine is that every rescued child must be given finally into the keeping of those of its own faith who will carry on the work begun in its rescue. Beyond that point the Society does not go. It has once refused the gift of a sea-side home lest it become a rival in a filed where it would render only friendly counsel and aid.

In the case of the little John Does, a doubt arises which the Society settles by passing them on to the best institution available for each particular child, quite irrespective of sect. There are thirteen of them by this time, waifs found in the street by the Society's agents or friends and never claimed by anybody. Though passed on, in the plan of the Society from which it never deviates, to be cared for by others, they are never lost sight of but always considered its special charges, for whom it bears a peculiar responsibility.

Poor Little Carmen, of whom I spoke of in the chapter about Italian children, was one of the Society's wards. Its footprints may be found all through these pages. To its [the Society's] printed reports, with their array of revolting cruelty and neglect, the reader is referred who would fully understand what a gap in a Christian community it bridges over.

21

Recent Articles and the Mary Ellen Songs

The following article was written by Dr. Stephen Lazoritz for the International Journal of Child Abuse and Neglect, September 1989:

WHATEVER HAPPENED TO MARY ELLEN?

By Dr. Stephen Lazoritz

Child Abuse & Neglect, September (1989): "Whatever Happened to Mary Ellen?" Vol 14, pp.143-149, Elsevier Science, Used with permission.

In June of 1936, a schoolteacher named Florence Brasser from a suburb of Rochester, New York, wrote a letter to Mr. John J. Smithers, general manager of the New York Society for the Prevention of Cruelty to Children. (NYSPCC) The reply came quickly. The stationery bore the official seal of the society, and in the space after the sentence, "In replying please refer to Case No. ____," the number "1" was neatly typed in.

"Dear Mrs. Brasser," the letter began, "You realize, I presume, that the epic story of 'Mary Ellen' is known throughout the civilized world, and it was the inspiration of the movement for the legal protection of children, not only in this country, but throughout the Universe at large."

Mary Ellen with daughters Florence (seated) and Etta. (Courtesy of the George Sim Johnston Archives of the NYSPCC.)

This might have been just another response to a request for information regarding the famous case of Mary Ellen, which resulted in the founding of the NYSPCC in 1874. However, in this instance the request was made by someone with more than just a passing interest in this case. It was made by Mary Ellen's youngest daughter, Florence.

Mr. Smithers' reply detailed to Florence how her grandmother, Frances (Fanny) Connor, came to the United States in 1858 from London, England. Frances married a soldier named Thomas Wilson, who died in the Civil War. In 1863, Frances Wilson wrote to her father that she was expecting a child, who was born that winter. Her mother abandoned the child, Mary Ellen, soon thereafter.

"The further circumstances you know, and it has been a profound satisfaction to this society to follow her later career, and to know that now, in the evening of her life, she has the comfort of daughters of whom she is proud," concluded Mr. Smithers.

Mr. Smithers was certainly correct in his statement that the case of Mary Ellen, and its profound and lasting effects on the cause of child protection, is universally known. The details of the rescue of Mary Ellen have been well chronicled elsewhere (Williams, 1880), but little has been written about the effect that this historic intervention had on the life of the victim of this terrible case of child abuse.

LIFE AFTER INTERVENTION

"What happened to little Mary Ellen?" asked Gertrude Williams (1980) in her chapter dealing with the plight of the little girl. "The former darling of the press, having served her purpose, was 'finally disposed of' by being reinstitutionalized."

When no suitable relatives could be found to care for her, Mary Ellen was placed in the Sheltering Arms, which was a home, not for young homeless children like herself, but one for adolescent girls, some of whom were troubled. Thus, the case of Mary Ellen was not only "the inspiration for the legal protection of children," but ironically it was also the first inappropriate placement resulting from such a case. (Wheeler, unknown).

Mrs. Etta Wheeler, the church worker from St. Luke's Methodist Mission, whose persistent efforts resulted in Mary Ellen's rescue, again came to the child's aid by expressing her disapproval with the placement at the Sheltering Arms to Judge Lawrence, who was Mary Ellen's guardian. Judge Lawrence put Mary Ellen at Mrs. Wheeler's disposal, and in June of 1875 the little girl was sent to live with Sally Angell, Etta Wheeler's mother, on a farm outside Rochester. Mrs. Angell died of tuberculosis in September of that year, and at her request, her youngest daughter, Elizabeth, and her husband, Darius W. Spencer, who lived nearby, raised Mary Ellen. (Wheeler, 1913).

THE PUBLICIZING OF MARY ELLEN

As Mary Ellen was beginning her new life, the public did not forget her life as an abused child. In the nation's centennial year76, a photograph of the ragged and beaten Mary Ellen was prominently displayed as part of the Society for the Prevention of Cruelty to Animals' exhibit at

Mary Ellen at an American Humane Association meeting, 1913.
(Courtesy of the George Sim Johnston Archives, NYSPCC)

the Philadelphia Centennial Exhibition, alongside specimens depicting other abused members of the animal kingdom. This exhibit was hardly popular, though, being described by the Philadelphia Times as "about as pleasant to the senses as an inspection of a thriving morgue in dog-days" (Steele, 1942).

During the same year as the Centennial, Henry P. Keens, a songwriter and composer of little renown, published two musical compositions based on the life of the abused child. The first, whose sheet music was graced with a photograph of the beaten and abused child, was titled "Little Mary Ellen" and was "dedicated by permission to Henry Bergh, Esq.", the president of the Society for the Prevention of Cruelty to Animals. This song (Keens, 1876) began:

> See within that dismal chamber
> Clothed in rags and chilled with fear
> No kind father to protect her
> With no watchful mother near
> Weeps an infant, pale and feeble,
> Victim of her keeper's rage,
> Tender flower crushed and broken,
> Blighted in her budding age.

And the chorus went:

> Who will help this little orphan
> Left on earth without a friend?
> Who will shelter and protect her?
> Who will peace and mercy send?

The second song (Keens, 1876), published simultaneously, was "dedicated by permission to Hon. Elbridge T. Gerry", who was Henry Bergh's attorney who argued on behalf of Mary Ellen. He later became the president of the Society for the Prevention of Cruelty to Children. Entitled "Mother Sent an Angel to Me," the cover of the sheet music bore a picture of Mary Ellen with her cheeks filled out and her wounds healed. It began:

> There in sweet repose reclining
> See a child of fairy grace
> Well might angels look with wonder
> On the beauty of her face
> Tell me, maiden, who has changed thee
> From what once thou used to be?
> Who has healed thy broken spirit
> Saved thee from captivity?

Sheet music for songs about Mary Ellen. (Courtesy of the George Sim Johnston Archives, NYSPCC.)

And the chorus:

Mother sent an angel to me
Clad in virtue's robe of white
Spreading wings of mercy o'er me
Made my darkest hour bright.

It is not known how popular these musical compositions were, but at least one critic described them to be "full of deep pathos" (Steele, 1942).

MARY ELLEN, THE SURVIVOR

Lewis Schutt, Mary Ellen's Husband.

Mary Ellen thrived in the Spencer home and attended school through grammar school. In 1888, at the age of 24, she married a widower of German heritage, Lewis Schutt. Mr. Schutt was a gentle, intelligent man with a huge handlebar mustache. He had worked as a railroad flagman and gardener and had two sons, Jesse and Clarence, by his former marriage. In April of 1897, Mary Ellen gave birth to her first daughter, Etta, named for Etta Wheeler, and four years later in May of 1901, she bore her second daughter, Florence.

The Schutt family was a poor but loving family. Mary Ellen loved music, especially Irish jigs. Her favorite was "The Irish Washerwoman," which would always get her to tap her feet. She also enjoyed singing hymns. Mary Ellen was known to collect little things, such as scraps of string. These little things meant a great deal to her. Mr. Schutt's German descent enabled him to help the children with their German homework, and Florence recalls regularly walking one and a half miles to the railroad crossing to bring her father his lunch.

Mary Ellen worked hard to care for her family and at one point, took in another child, Eunice, to care for as a foster child for many years. Though she was not active in the child protection movement, Mary Ellen did attend the 37th Annual Meeting of the American Humane Association that was held in Rochester in October 1913.

Mary Ellen's daughter, Florence Brasser, with Mary Ellen's trunk.

At that meeting, Mrs. Etta Wheeler presented a paper entitled, "The Finding of Mary Ellen," in which she described her role in the rescue of the abused child

303

(Meeting announcement, 1913).

RECOLLECTIONS OF MARY ELLEN BY HER FAMILY

When her children and grandchildren would ask Mary Ellen about her childhood in New York, she would try to change the topic. "I suppose she had enough of it," reflected Florence. But Mary Ellen did provide some details of her miserable existence. She described Mrs. Connolly, her stepmother who brutalized her, as a "mean looking woman". Florence remembers her mother telling her of an incident when her mother was drying some clothes, and "she (Mrs. Connolly) got mad at something and took the hot iron and put it right on her (Mary Ellen's) arm . . . that was a burn!"

Florence described seeing scars on her mother, "on her arms wherever she hurt her." Eunice remembers scars

Mary Ellen Schutt, circa 1923.
(Courtesy Helen Finlayson.)

around Mary Ellen's left eye, which were caused when Mrs. Connolly hit her on the face with scissors. "Grandma never knew when she would be punished, or for what, or how greatly," recalled Etta's daughter, Shirley Mehlenbacher.

Mary Ellen's daughter and granddaughter described Mary Ellen as being not much of a disciplinarian. "It wasn't her nature to spank very much. She might threaten you, but she would rarely do it." Florence described her mother as always wanting her to "be good and do the right thing." If they

Eunice & Florence. (Courtesy, Helen Finlayson)

weren't? "She just punished us, that's all. Just spank us and that's as hard as it went. She would spank our little bottom." Eunice agreed that bad behavior might result in an occasional spanking, "but she had to catch me first," and recalled outrunning her foster mother. "She was just a real sweet lady."

FAMILY ACHIEVEMENTS

Perhaps the most remarkable and gratifying aspects of Mary Ellen's life were the accomplishments of her daughters. Both Etta and Florence attended college and

Florence and Etta at Thomas Wilson's grave. (Courtesy Helen Finlayson.)

became teachers. Etta was a well-respected teacher in the Rochester Public Schools. She had a deep love for working with children, and her teaching career spanned thirty-nine years. She died in 1988 at the age of 91.

Florence also had a long teaching career, thirty-seven years, but one in which she achieved a unique honor. In 1955, Chili School 11, where she had taught since 1928,

Florence A. Brasser School, named after Mary Ellen's daughter – while she still taught there. (Photo by Eric A. Shelman)

was officially named the Florence Brasser School in her honor. She continued to teach at the school that bore her name until her retirement in 1961. In 1967 the New York State Legislature recognized Mrs. Brasser for her lifelong accomplishments with a resolution in her honor. Mrs. Brasser died in 1992, also at the age of 91.

Mary Ellen herself died on October 3056, at the age of 92. Those of us who work for the protection of abused and neglected children, however, will always remember her as she was in 1874; a child in need of protection and the inspiration for a revolution in her country's concern for children. But perhaps we should take a new look at Mary Ellen. We should look at the child who was able to thrive in a loving environment and to grow into an adult who had children of whom she was proud. Perhaps we should see Mary Ellen not as the victim of abuse, but as the survivor, and as a persistent reminder that the efforts of a few people on behalf of one child can make a real difference.

Mary Ellen Schutt – Age Unknown. (Courtesy of the George Sim Johnston Archives, NYSPCC.)

This article was written by a great admirer of Etta Wheeler. So much so, the author submitted Etta's name as an inductee candidate for the National Women's Hall of Fame.

HER HEART WENT OUT TO ONE CHILD, ALL CHILDREN
By Lisa Van Leeuwen

One hundred and thirty-eight years ago, a local woman instigated a worldwide movement that would profoundly change the way children are treated under the law.

While ministering to the poor in New York City's Hell's Kitchen, Ogden native Etta Angell Wheeler was told that a little girl in one of the buildings was being brutalized on a daily basis.

Etta investigated, knocking on the door of the apartment where the little girl lived. When a woman opened the door, Etta began talking while covertly scanning the apartment for a glimpse of the tortured child.

Balancing on a pan set on top of a stool, the child struggled to wash a huge pan. Though it was winter, she was nearly naked. A horsewhip lay nearby, and Etta's eyes were drawn to the slashes and scars on the girl's tiny limbs from its use. Pale and malnourished, the little girl had the stature of a 5-year-old, though it was later determined that she was then 9.

"These things I saw while seeming not to see," Etta later wrote, "and left without speaking to, or of, the child."

Determined to end this cruelty, Etta sought help from various authorities, to no avail. A child was thought lucky to have any roof over his or her head, no matter what horrors occurred beneath it. Months passed as Etta continued to visit the tenements and monitor the child's situation from a neighbor's apartment.

Frustrated and deeply saddened by the suffering child, Etta had considered appealing to the Society for the Prevention of Cruelty to Animals, but, in her own words, "lacked the courage to do what seemed absurd."

But when a niece said, "You are so troubled over that abused child, why not go to Mr. Bergh? She is a little animal, surely," Etta went at once to the SPCA founder's office.

Henry Bergh expressed interest in helping, but stated that careful documentation would be needed to justify intervention. She immediately drafted case testimony.

The brilliance of this document cannot be overstated. It contained not only a detailed description of the situation, but also the very legal grounds upon which the child would be freed.

Included in the statement was the following. "The landlady of this house … asserts that Mrs. Connolly told her … the little girl Mary Ellen was not her child nor her husband's …"

Bergh summoned his lawyer, Elbridge Gerry, and on April 9, 1874, Mary Ellen was removed from the home on a writ of habeas corpus (false imprisonment).

Appall at Mary Ellen's initial placement in a home for wayward girls, Etta obtained custody herself, sending Mary Ellen to live with her parents on Buffalo Road in Ogden. When Etta's mother died shortly thereafter, Etta's sister, Elizabeth and her husband, Chili Town Justice Darius W. Spencer, raised Mary Ellen.

Though Mary Ellen was now well cared for, Etta was well aware that many other children endured similarly dire situations. She approached Bergh again, asserting that there must be a "society which does for children what is being so well done to animals." Bergh replied, "There shall be one."

In 1875, the Society for the Prevention of Cruelty to Children was formed in New York City by Bergh, Gerry, and John D. Wright. The Rochester chapter opened the next year.

As testimony to the effectiveness of early intervention, Mary Ellen grew up happy, married Lewis Schutt, a railroad worker from the town of Greece, NY, and raised two daughters. One of them, teacher Florence Brasser (nee Schutt) so impressed her colleagues at Chili School no 11, that the school is now named Florence Brasser Elementary School.

Etta devoted herself fully to SPCC's work and was entitled a lifetime member, an honor shared with Ulysses S. Grant and John D. Lindsay. Her status as a woman, however, resulted in most of the credit for SPCC's founding going to the more press-savvy and political-minded Bergh and Gerry.

Today, the caring souls at Lollypop Farm and the SPCC on South Fitzhugh Street carry on the important work on behalf of children and animals begun by Wheeler and Bergh, and understand the depth of this area's roots in the anti-cruelty movement.

Yet, the name of this hometown heroine remains virtually unknown to local historians. Why?

The worldwide attention on Mary Ellen's case necessitated keeping her new home here confidential. So, there could be no hero's welcome when Etta returned from New York. Nor was she lauded in the local press, for the same reason.

This month, a National Women's Hall of Fame nomination will be submitted for Etta Angell Wheeler.

Case #1: The Mary Ellen Wilson Files

Like many women of her time, credit for much of Etta's heartfelt work was lavished on the men around her. I hope that Etta will finally claim her rightful place among our U.S. heroines.

Van Leeuwen, of Churchville, is majoring in psychology with a minor in journalism at the University of Rochester.

Mary Ellen Schutt – Photo date unknown. (Courtesy Helen Finlayson.)

Mary Ellen Schutt in 1946. (Courtesy Helen Finlayson)

Last known photograph of Mary Ellen, taken in 1955.
(Courtesy of Helen Finlayson.)

GRATITUDE

We've relied heavily on others to provide us with information about Mary Ellen and her family. The photos of Mary Ellen and her family, provided by Helen Finlayson and Frank Mehlenbacher, are priceless. At the mention of Frank, we must also mention his wife, Shirley Mehlenbacher, Etta Pease's daughter, who signed the first letter of authorization, allowing us to obtain the crucial court transcripts contained herein. Stephen Zawistowski, PhD., of the American Society for the Prevention of Cruelty to Animals (ASPCA) was instrumental to our research on Bergh. Any time we needed anything, he was responsive, supportive, and downright eager to help! On the other side of this over century old fence, we owe nearly everything to the New York Society for the Prevention of Cruelty to Children (NYSPCC), in particular, Joseph Gleason. He is the archivist at the society, and performed research, pulled and copied delicate documents and photos, and basically made much of this and our last book

Gravestone of Mary Ellen and Lewis Schutt. (Mary Ellen's birth year was modified by the family due to information learned by the authors.)

possible. At his side for a time, was Anne Reiniger, former Executive Director of the NYSPCC. She also helped us succeed in our mission. After Anne's tenure as Director, we had the pleasure of being assisted by her replacement, Mary Pulido, MAT, CSW. While there are a number of people to thank, the individuals above stand out among them, and deserve individual recognition. We'd like to thank Guardian Ad Litem (GAL) and Court Appointed Special Advocate (CASA) volunteers all over the country. You make a tremendous difference in the lives of abused, abandoned, and neglected children and your work should be recognized and applauded. Bravo.

Appendix A

Sheet Music for Songs About Mary Ellen

(Courtesy of the George Sim Johnston Archives of the NYSPCC.)

HENRY BERGH, ESQ.

Little Mary Ellen.

Rescued from the woman Coinolly in 1874 by the officers of the American Society for the prevention of cruelty to Animals.

Song and Chorus

Words and Music by

Henry P. Keens.

NEW YORK
PUBLISHED BY Wm A. POND & CO, 547 BROADWAY
AND 39 UNION SQUARE

319

LITTLE MARY ELLEN.

SONG AND CHORUS.

Words & Music by HENRY P. KEERNS.

Moderato.

1. See   with - in that dis- mal cham- ber,   Clothed in rags and chilled with fear...
2. See   up - on her trembling bod - y,   How the blows fall thick and fast...
3. Why should this poor sin - less crea - ture,   Pine in sor - row ev - 'ry hour?..

0270

4

No kind fa-ther to pro-tect her__ With no watchful mother near....
Till her life in ling'ring tor-ture, Slow-ly ebbs a-way at last....
Ling'ring on till death, a cap-tive To her heartless ruler's pow-er?

rit.

Weeps an in-fant pale and fee-ble, Vic-tim of her keeper's rage....
Fa-ther!moth-er!look from Heav-en, On the off-spring of your love....
Are there none with hearts of pit-y, Who will shel-ter her with love?...

a tempo.

Ten-der flow-er crush'd and bro-ken, Blight-ed in her budding age....
Bid the An-gels on their pin-ions, Bear her gent-ly up a-bove....
Who will save her from de-struc-tion, Bear-ing mercy from a-bove?...

0270

* The above can also be sung as a solo without diminishing the effect.

HON. ELBRIDGE T. GERRY.

Mother sent an Angel to me.

Answer to "LITTLE MARY ELLEN", who is now in her new home.

Song and Chorus

Words and Music by

Henry P. Keens.

NEW YORK
PUBLISHED BY Wm. A. POND & CO. 547 BROADWAY
AND 39 UNION SQUARE

MILWAUKEE,   SAN FRANCISCO,   BOSTON,   CINCINNATI O.,   NEW ORLEANS
H. N. HEMPSTED   M. GRAY   CARL PRUFER,   C. Y. FONDA,   L. GRUNEWALD.

W. TELLER, 40 CHURCH ST. N. YORK

3

MOTHER SENT AN ANGEL TO ME.

SONG AND CHORUS.

Words & Music by HENRY P. KEENS.

0271

4

Well might Angels look with won - der
On the beau-ty of her face!..
Tran - quil peace and sweet con - tent - ment,
Love and mer-cy ev' - ry - where..
For the Agents of the Fa - ther,
Sent in mer-cy from a - bove:..

accelerando.

"Tell me, maiden, who has changed thee
From what once thou used to be?....
Heark - en to the mer - ry laugh - ter,
See how bright the sparkling eye ....
Breathe a si-lent pray'r for par - don,
On that cul-prit's guil-ty head ...

poco rit.

Who has healed thy bro-ken spir - it___
Saved thee from cap-tiv - i - ty?"....
Now no more the youthful bo - som
Ut - ters forth the plain-tive cry....
Who had well-nigh had thee numbered,
With the spir - its of the dead!..

9271

*CHORUS.
5
SOP.
ALTO.
TENOR.
BASS.
PIANO.
Mother sent an Angel to me, Clad in Virtue's robe of white...
Mother sent an Angel to me, Clad in Virtue's robe of white...
ff
pp
Spreading wings of mer-cy o'er me, Made my darkest hour bright...
Spreading wings of mer-cy o'er me, Made my darkest hour bright...
0271
*The above can be sung either as a Solo or Chorus.

Appendix B

The Counts Against Mary Connolly

(Courtesy of the George Sim Johnston Archives of the NYSPCC.)

Case #1: The Mary Ellen Wilson Files

CITY AND COUNTY
OF NEW YORK, } *ss.*

THE JURORS OF THE PEOPLE OF THE STATE OF NEW YORK,

*in and for the body of the City and County of New York,
upon their oath, present:*

That *Mary Connolly*

late of the City of New York, in the County of New York, aforesaid,

on the *Seventh* day of *April* in the year of our Lord one thousand eight hundred and seventy-*four* with force and arms, at the City and County aforesaid, in and upon the body *of a certain female child called Mary Ellen* in the peace of the said people then and there being, feloniously did make an assault and *her* the said *female child called Mary Ellen* with a certain *scissors* which the said *Mary Connolly* in *her* right hand then and there had and held, the same being a deadly and dangerous weapon, wilfully and feloniously did beat, strike, stab, cut, and wound, with intent *her* the said *female child called Mary Ellen* then and there, feloniously and wilfully to kill, against the form of the Statute in such case made and provided, and against the peace of the People of the State of New York, and their dignity.

SECOND COUNT.

And the Jurors aforesaid, upon their Oaths aforesaid, do further present: That afterwards, to wit, on the day and in the year aforesaid, at the City and County aforesaid, the said *Mary Connolly* with force and arms, in and upon the body of the said *female child called Mary Ellen* then and there being, wilfully and feloniously did make another assault and *her* the said *female child called Mary Ellen* with a certain *scissors* which the said *Mary Connolly* in *her* right hand, then and there had and held, the same being then and there a sharp, dangerous weapon, wilfully and feloniously, and without justifiable and excusable cause, did then and there beat, strike, stab, cut, and wound, with intent to then and there wilfully and feloniously do bodily harm unto *her* the said *female child called Mary Ellen* against the form of the Statute in such case made and provided, and against the peace of the People of the State of New York and their dignity.

And the Jurors aforesaid upon their Oath aforesaid, do further present : That afterwards, to wit, on the day and in the year aforesaid, at the City and County aforesaid the said *Mary Connolly* with force and arms, in and upon the body of *certain female child called Mary Ellen* , in the peace of the said people then and there being, feloniously did make another assault and *her* the said *female child called Mary Ellen* with a certain *a scissor* which the said *Mary Connolly* in *her* right hand then and there had and held, wilfully and feloniously did beat, strike, stab, cut, and wound, the same being such means and force as was likely to produce the death of *her* the said *female child called Mary Ellen* with intent *her* the said *female child called Mary Ellen* then and there feloniously and wilfully to kill, against the form of the Statute in such case made and provided, and against the peace of the People of the State of New York and their dignity.

FOURTH COUNT.

And the Jurors aforesaid, upon their Oath aforesaid, do further present : That afterwards, to wit, on the day and in the year aforesaid, at the City and County aforesaid, the said *Mary Connolly* with force and arms, in and upon the body of the said *female child called Mary Ellen* , then and there being, wilfully and feloniously did make another assault and *her* the said *female child called Mary Ellen* with a certain *scissor* which the said *Mary Connolly* in *her* right hand then and there had and held, the same being then and there a deadly weapon, wilfully and feloniously did then and there beat, strike, stab, cut, and wound, with intent to then and there wilfully and feloniously maim *her* the said *female child called Mary Ellen* against the form of the Statute in such case made and provided, and against the peace of the People of the State of New York and their dignity.

Seventh Count

And the Jurors aforesaid upon their Oath aforesaid, do further present: That afterwards, to wit, on the day and in the year aforesaid, at the City and County aforesaid the said *Mary Connolly* with force and arms, in and upon the body of *Mary Ellen Wilson*, in the peace of the said people then and there being, feloniously did make another assault and the said *Mary Ellen Wilson* with a certain *scissors* which the said *Mary Connolly* in her right hand then and there had and held, willfully and feloniously did beat, strike, stab, cut, and wound, the same being such means and force as was likely to produce the death of her the said *Mary Ellen Wilson* with intent her the said *Mary Ellen Wilson* then and there feloniously and willfully to kill, against the form of the Statute in such case made and provided, and against the peace of the People of the State of New York and their dignity.

Eighth Count.

And the Jurors aforesaid, upon their Oath aforesaid, do further present: That afterwards, to wit, on the day and in the year aforesaid, at the City and County aforesaid, the said *Mary Connolly* with force and arms, in and upon the body of the said *Mary Ellen Wilson*, then and there being, willfully and feloniously did make another assault and her the said *Mary Ellen Wilson* with a certain *scissors* which the said *Mary Connolly* in her right hand then and there had and held, the same being then and there a deadly weapon, willfully and feloniously did then and there beat, strike, stab, cut, and wound, with intent to then and there willfully and feloniously maim her the said *Mary Ellen Wilson* against the form of the Statute in such case made and provided, and against the peace of the People of the State of New York and their dignity.

CITY AND COUNTY
OF NEW YORK
aforesaid

THE JURORS OF THE PEOPLE OF THE STATE OF NEW YORK,
in and for the body of the City and County of New York,
upon their oath, present aforesaid d of in the present

ninth Count

That *Mary Connolly*

late of the City of New York, in the County of New York, aforesaid,

on the *second* day of *April* in the year of our Lord
one thousand eight hundred and seventy *four* with force and arms, at the City and
County aforesaid, in and upon the body of *Mary Ellen McCormack*
in the peace of the said people then and there being, feloniously did make an assault
and *her* the said *Mary Ellen McCormack* which
with a certain *scissor*

the said *Mary Connolly*

in *her* right hand then and there had and held, the same being a deadly and
dangerous weapon, wilfully and feloniously did beat, strike, stab, cut and wound,
with intent *her* the said *Mary Ellen McCormack*
then and there, feloniously and wilfully to kill, against the form of the Statute in such
case made and provided, and against the peace of the People of the State of New
York, and their dignity.

Tenth Count
SECOND COUNT

And the Jurors aforesaid, upon their Oath aforesaid, do further present: That
afterwards, to wit, on the day and in the year aforesaid, at the City and County afore
said, the said *Mary Connolly* and *Mary Ellen McCormack*
with force and arms, in and upon the body of the said *Mary Ellen McCormack*
then and there being, wilfully and feloniously did make another
assault and *her* the said *Mary Ellen McCormack*
with a certain *scissor*
which the said *Mary Connolly*

in *her* right hand, then and there had and held, the same being
then and there a sharp, dangerous weapon, wilfully and feloniously, and without
justifiable and excusable cause, did then and there beat, strike, stab, cut, and wound,
with intent to then and there wilfully and feloniously do bodily harm unto
her the said *Mary Ellen McCormack* against the form of the
Statute in such case made and provided, and against the peace of the People of the
State of New York and their dignity.

Eleventh Count

And the Jurors aforesaid upon their Oath aforesaid, do further present: That afterwards, to wit, on the day and in the year aforesaid, at the City and County aforesaid the said *Mary Connolly* with force and arms, in and upon the body of *Mary Ellen McCormack*, in the peace of the said people then and there being feloniously did make another assault and *her* the said *Mary Ellen McCormack* with a certain *Scissors* which the said *Mary Connolly* in *her* hand then and there had and held, wilfully and feloniously did beat, strike, stab, cut, and wound, the same being such means and have, as was likely to produce the death of *her* the said *Mary Ellen McCormack* with intent *her* the said *Mary Ellen McCormack* then and there feloniously and wilfully to kill, against the form of the Statute in such case made and provided, and against the peace of the People of the State of New York and their dignity.

Twelfth Count

And the Jurors aforesaid, upon their Oath aforesaid, do further present: That afterwards, to wit, on the day and in the year aforesaid, at the City and County aforesaid, the said *Mary Connolly* with force and arms, in and upon the body of the said *Mary Ellen McCormack* then and there being, wilfully and feloniously did make another assault and *her* the said *Mary Ellen McCormack* with a certain *Scissors* which the said *Mary Connolly* in *her* right hand then and there had and held, the same being then and there a deadly weapon, wilfully and feloniously did then and there beat, strike, stab, cut, and wound, with intent to then and there wilfully and feloniously main *her* the said *Mary Ellen McCormack* against the form of the Statute in such case made and provided, and against the peace of the People of the State of New York and their dignity.

B. K. PHELPS, District Attorney

Bibliography

New York Society for the Prevention of Cruelty to Children (NYSPCC) (1874) Mary Ellen Wilson file (with permission granted to authors by Wilson descendants)

Bonner, Robert (1867) The New York Ledger

Buel, C.C. (1879), "Henry Bergh and His Work" Scribner's Magazine, April

Buffalo Daily Courier (1874)

Buffett, Edward P. (192?) Unpublished notes provided courtesy of the American Society for the Prevention of Cruelty to Animals (ASPCA)

Delille, H.A. (1866) Home Journal

Finlayson, Helen (Photographs)

Lazoritz, Stephen (1990), Whatever Happened To Mary Ellen, International Journal of Child Abuse and Neglect, Milwaukee, S.143-149

Lazoritz, Stephen/**Shelman** Eric (1996), Before Mary Ellen, International Journal of Child Abuse and Neglect, Milwaukee, WI

Mehlenbacher, Frank & Shirley Photos and Permissions

New York Daily Tribune (1867-1875)

New York Evening Post (1874)

New York Herald (1867-1875)

New York Sun (1867)

New York Telegram (1868)

New York Times (1867-1875)

Riis, Jacob A. (1890) How the Other Half Lives, New York

Riis, Jacob A. (1892) Children of the Poor, New York

Steele, Zulma (1942), Angel in Top Hat, New York

Stevens, Peter/**Eide**, Marian (1990), The First Chapter of Children's Rights, American Heritage, July/August, S.84-91

The New York Ledger (1867)

The Northern Budget (1867) Troy, NY

The People Vs. Mary Connolly (1874), Indictment Papers, Case nos 1261/1262, New York Municipal Archives, Department of Records and Information Services

Van Leeuwen, Lisa (July 1100) Essay, Her heart went out to one child, all children, Democrat and Chronicle, S.7A, Rochester, NY

Wallace, Irving/**Wallechinsky**, David/**Wallace**, Amy (1983), Significa, New York

Wheeler, Etta Angell (1913), "The Case of Mary Ellen" as told by her Rescuer E.A. Wheeler, The National Humane Review, Vol. 1, August , No. 8

Index

(Note: These index references have no page numbers, so suggest you use the Table Of Contents unless a digital version of this book, and in that case these are provided more for search terms. *Initials* ME *denote* Mary Ellen.